The Uninvited Season

The Uninvited Season

A Literary Memorial to
Kimberley Elizabeth Sherman Grove

Editor
Prof. Miguel Ángel Olivé Iglesias. MSc

First Edition

Wet Ink Books
www.WetInkBooks.com
WetInkBooks@gmail.com

The Uninvited Season:
A Literary Memorial to Kimberley Elizabeth Sherman Grove

Editor – Miguel Ángel Olivé Iglesias
Cover Design – Richard M. Grove
Cover Image – Richard M. Grove
Layout and Design – Richard M. Grove

Typeset in Garamond
Printed and bound in Canada
Distributed in USA by Ingram,
           – to set up an account – 1-800-937-0152

Library and Archives Canada Cataloguing in Publication

Title: The uninvited season : a literary memorial to Kimberley Elizabeth Sherman Grove / editor,   Prof. Miguel Ángel Olivé Iglesias, MSc.
Other titles: Uninvited season (Compilation)
Names: Grove, Kimberley, 1956-2024, author. | Olivé Iglesias, Miguel Ángel, 1965- editor, author.
Identifiers: Canadiana 20250219433 | ISBN 9781998324217 (softcover)
Subjects: LCSH: Grove, Kimberley, 1956-2024—Criticism and interpretation. | CSH: Authors, Canadian (English)—21st century. | LCGFT: Festschriften. | LCGFT: Commemorative works. | LCGFT:
    Literature.
Classification: LCC PS8613.R7465 Z8 2025 | DDC C818/.609—dc23

Dedicated to,

dear Kim, with all of our gratitude for her indelible and beautiful presence in our lives. She brightened many lives in so many ways. —she revivified people´s lives simply by being Kim.

She will be remembered in words and deeds.

Contents

Selected Poems by Kimberley Grove

Selected Prose by Kimberley Grove

Tribute Writings to Kim

Essays about Kim's Poetry

Acknowledgments

As Editor I wish to thank first and foremost Richard M. Grove (Tai). His confidence in me to work on this special volume is heartwarming. He has entrusted me with the writing, translation and edition of many other books during our almost decade of cooperation. However, all of you, readers, will agree that this one carries an extra touch of love and dedication.

I thank all of the authors who sent their poems and comments to pay tribute to Kim. The Canada Caribbean Literary Alliance, *The Envoy* newsletter, collected them for its special issue, but Kim´s legacy and motivations reach out beyond the newsletter´s pages and flow river-like to this book.

I thank my coeditor, Jorge Alberto Pérez Hernández. His close friendship with Kim added more significance to our endevour.

An Important Thank You

Thank you dear Miguel. You live up to the nick name of being my Wingman. Thank you my dear friend for your commitment to this wonderful Kim CanLit book that you have assembled with such love and generosity. My heart was too broken to take on the job that you were so willing to take on. Thank you from the bottom of my heart for such a fine collection of Kim's work.

Richard M. Grove / Tai

A Poetry Preface from Richard Grove (Tai), Kim's husband

The Uninvited Season

The uninvited season arrived,
unwritten, blank pages in a well-read,
dog-eared poetry book, a new chapter slipped
between spring's green breath of freshness
and winter's tranquil repose. I am learning
this uninvited season need not be cold
or filled with storms of thrashing waves and fog.
It is up to you. It can arrive as
a soft whisper of fluttering butterfly wings,
reminding us all about eternity,
a statement that one is loved by Love itself.
The mist lifts to reveal the timelessness of now
that brings peace and assurance that all is well
in the silent uninvited season of infinity.

In this season, the space that once seemed
too wide to cross, like the shadows stretching
at dusk, begins to shrink and fade
the unfulfilled expectations of grief.
The hand-holding distance on the sofa,
became a chasm with your passing,
seeming too wide to cross, will now shrink
and vanish. The invisible space between us
is not emptiness but finally a connection
beyond form, where heartbeats are never lost
in silence, and love is unbroken.

It is not just the warmth of your hand that I miss,
but the simple weight of seeming reality
pressed in mine. I reach for you
through the uninvited season, reaching,
and finding you are still and always will be
the perfect reflection and expression
of divine Life's living despite the unrequited touch.

My understanding is now filled
with the presence of all that you are,
a spiritual being,
the never-ending vibrancy of the real you.
This uninvited season is not a season of endings,
but a season of moving forward, a bridge to eternity.

Though a silent whisper, this uninvited season
will fill the blank pages of the untitled chapters
yet to come and fill tomorrow's expectations
with the joy of light filling the ether
with the perfume of beginnings.
This is not an end, but a beginning where we both
will enjoy the silent joy-filled journey
from harmony, through harmony, to harmony
as I free myself from the earth bound illusion
of my unfulfilled expectations.

Pure, Upright, Whole and Free

For Kim

I was thinking about how amazing you were
through this seemingly
long process before you passed on.
There was never, absolutely never,
any whining, crying, moaning or bemoaning.
What an incredibly fearless, courageous,
demonstration of joy you were, you are.

Do you remember my brother Chris
had a nickname for you?
He called you "Intrepid"
because of your willingness to march forward
in the face of adversity
no matter what was put in front of you.
In your courage you were valiant and brave,
undisturbed.

In our prayers together
we kept repeating that you are;
Pure, Upright, Whole and Free.
Pure, Upright, Whole and Free.
That is how divine Law has always known you.
That is how I still think of you my Dove;
Pure, Upright, Whole and Free,
now and always, never any
whining, crying, moaning or bemoaning.
I am amazed and proud of you for your courage.

Introduction by the Editor

This is a book with, about and for Kimberley Elizabeth Sherman Grove—our Kim. Her husband, Richard (Tai) Grove, generously asked me to be the editor of a book that would collect in a single volume much of her literary writings and the wholehearted words of tribute her husband, friends and acquaintances gratefully wrote to our indelible Kim. I was deeply honoured.

Lingering gently and sweetly in her own special aura, Kim wrote poetry and prose capturing with singular insightfulness and sentience what was around her. Particularly keen, in my view, are her poems to nature—that deeply rooted *leitmotif* virtue Canadian poets carry in their blood—where we perceive her profound connection, which I revealed in my poems and my essays on her work.

The November issue of *The Envoy* 129 (the Canada Caribbean Literary Alliance newsletter), edited by Jorge Pérez from Gibara, Cuba, was fully dedicated to Kim. I wrote the words below for her:

A Word of Tribute
to a Woman of High Praise

We have lost someone dear to us all. The so called material law of life dictated so. With the loss of Canadian writer, beloved wife and friend Kimberley Elizabeth Sherman Grove, life darkens for many friends, family, colleagues. Yet amidst the sorrow we stand to honour her life and her achievements. Kim enjoyed writing since she first picked up a pencil. Her enchantment with Cuba was profoundly linked to her love of poetry. Kim visited Cuba, with her husband, every year for over twenty-five years. She published in The Globe and Mail, Christian Science Monitor, Toronto Star and various other publications. She taught writing at Loyalist College, the Trenton Air Force Base, the Colborne Community Care Centre and Ciego de Avila University in Cuba. Her teaching came from a love of reading what others have to share. She was also included in many anthologies published by Hidden Brook Press and SandCrab Books. May my heartfelt words pay homage to a generous, patient, smiling woman who lit up anyone's life simply with her presence.

How painful is life when someone close sadly passes on? How much does their physical absence affect us? For us, Kimberley Elizabeth Sherman Grove is not gone. That is impossible. Kim's metaphysical understanding of life is that life is eternal and her human, post-passing-existence does not depend on the remembrance of others. From her perspective, her Kimness still exists as Kim, though out of sight in some ethereal way. From my perspective, no one really leaves us if their acts in this life reached and touched our lives in ways words cannot express. In the necessary moment of celebrating a life of joy and caring, we are blessed by and rejoice in the unique blend of simplicity, because Kim was a humble woman, and of greatness, because she was the epitome of great, enveloped in her subtle yet transcendent behaviour. Physicality fills us, yes, and when it ends, it hurts deeply. But Kim's absence finds some sort of peace within us thanks to the spirituality that always surrounded her and the Divine that dwelt inside her.

Kim lingers on in the ever-ether of the Eternal. That is how we must remember her and visualize her bright presence: from a higher, thankful perspective that somehow lightens the anguish of her parting. Kim wondered at the idea of infinity. One of her poems reveals it:

> What is it about the ocean?
> That draws me to its shore?
> Is it the lulling of the waves?
> Swaying the shifting sand?
> Or the dramatic slapping,
> Clapping sound of water making war?
> No, I think it is the
> Openness of the ocean's wide embrace
> That draws me to stand on the cliffs' shoulders
> To see Infinity's face.

Her eyes and soul absorbing the magic of the ocean and the mystery of infinity, Kim leaves for us a poem of admiration and awe, of humility and veneration. That is our Kim, the poet, the profound human being. She wondrously holds now in her the answers to her questions.

I invite you to approach this book with the same kind of love Kim professed when she privileged us with her presence, her tenderness, her friendship. There is no other way.

Prof. Miguel Ángel Olivé Iglesias. MSc

Selected Poems
by Kimberley Grove

A Reader's prayer

Feast of God
I am but the humble server
Congregation come to be fed
In their best dress of giving attitude
And then we can say grace

Infinity

What is it about the ocean
That draws me to its shore?
Is it the lulling of the waves
swaying the shifting sand?
Or the dramatic slapping,
clapping sound of water
making war?
No, I think it is the
Openness of the ocean's
wide embrace
That draws me to stand
on the cliff's shoulders
To see Infinity's face.

A Walk in Winter

Through drifts of snow I plod
treading softly in your large footprints
as though only one of us is here.
Our soundless steps in snow
moved from the forest's powdered wisps
to the open crispness
creaking like Styrofoam under our feet.
Back towards the woods, the snow has drawn
lines on slender trunks of skunk-backed trees.
Gazing ahead to a blue Wedgewood sky,
the lake's edge is lined with winter pyramids.
Our blue shadows casting tall images,
I reach up to kiss you, my explorer,
but the icy wetness of your moustache
is like rubbing noses with a walrus.
The menagerie lies tucked among moon craters.
Overhanging where water used to be,
iced-over branches, glass drippings
extend fragile antlers.
Along a path, tangled snow-skeins
run their wool. A great mound
of woven ice strands drape
a lion's mane over the rocks.
Near the shore a snowdrift polar bear is resting.
Icy fangs protruding from the troubled water's edge
appear like elephant tusks, not needing to be whitened.
A fallen branch at the base of a tree
a teeter-totter for two well-balanced friends.
You and I sit staring at the Arctic scene
sharing a carrot popsicle as an iceberg swan
glides by gracefully.
We stay to marvel until we fear
we will become frozen sculptures.

Nature's Needlepoint

The view from my cabin window
is Nature's large empty cloth.
White as this page, winter lingers.
Brittle frosted branches
begin the lines and angles
etching a rough gray sketch
with the needle's single trail.
Spring's streaks of lightning
startle any artist's hand
as the rumbling thunder like distant fireworks
warns that the belly of the sky will open.
The artist's cloth is rinsed through
before jungle shades of green
begin to border the scene.
Then the whistle of a camouflaged thrush
pierces the air; the sound struggles, reaching
for sunlight to signal summer's lazy days.
Bright yellow daffodils worship the sun
while lilacs perfume the air.
Roses, lilies and tulips
sew more colour into the fabric.
She adds the hundreds of leaves
that will crumple underfoot
like worn paper bags.
The height of colour woven into Her work,
She applies some final touches, blowing away
unnecessary edges or redoing ugly patches.
A sewn-in signature
like the branding of a great creature,
the artisan stands back with me
to survey the masterpiece.

Home I

They opened their doors
Welcoming me into their souls
I was a stranger when I came
A sister when I left

One told me of losing her family
Not in a forest or losing them in a city
But losing them all in one small bunker
When the Nazis covered up the air pipes
Of their hiding place
"Why the heck did you wake me?
I was happy sleeping,"
she told the doctor that revived her
The only survivor.

Another smiled at a memory
Of the first time she met her husband
He was a Polish soldier and he asked her
"Little girl, do you like my shiny buttons?"
"No, I like you," she replied.

The one small pocket of light, of hope
Were the young Russian prisoners of war
That marched each day
inside the Auschwitz gates
The young women finally
had something to look forward to
And there was little else in those dark days
When the doors were locked
and the smell of burning flesh
Sickened these same young women
My new friend said,
"I couldn't help but think a 1,000 mothers
were crying in Russia that day."

Another told of what it was like
when the war was over
"We had to learn
not to be afraid of being afraid."
Another said, "I was embarrassed to tell people.
Both my parents survived."

They all had different stories
But one thing was the same
Despite what had been taken from them
They never lost a sense of home
Evil couldn't touch their consciousness
However much it might have tried
And those who survived best
Were those who learned
To rid their homes of hate.

Home II

Home is not a place
It is a secure thought
So deeply rooted
That it can't be dug up
Overturned or loosened
It is the quiet assurance
That all is well

Home III

They took me to a place
That wasn't pleasant
Filled with sad memories
Windows had been shut for many years
Doors only slightly opened
Because they could not
Allow further pain
Into their weary souls
All that was left of their lives
Was a foundation, but it was solid
They didn't speak of hate
They didn't speak of war
They spoke of loved ones gone
Of adopted grandparents for their children
Photos of grand and great grand children
Filled every walls and voices with such pride
They survived to tell us how to live
To teach us that home is in our heart
Never to be extinguished.

This Hand

Clenched tightly in a fist of rage
Another UN resolution
Tossed against the wall
A ball of false promises
This crumpled paper
Is picked up again
And the whiteness unfolds
Like the opening of a bud
As the fingers loosen, easing slowly
The number six million, branded,
Etched harshly in the open flesh
In the palm of this hand
Reaching, stretching forth
Not for you or me
But to shake hands
with the enemy

His Creativity

His creativity was in a fragile moment
If I moved, tried to eat my dinner
Enjoy a conversation, then
I was an interruption,
A disruption, an eruption
From our caring and sharing
That we usually foster
When eating out
Was I offended?
Sometimes yes, but I mended.

Northern Memories

Summer began with the first speck
of distant blue that would ignite
a carload of children's chorus,
chanting almost mechanically,
"I see the lake, and the lake sees me."
When the car finally stopped,
to our parent's relief
we'd disrobe to our bathing suits,
jumping out of the old Duster
with such force that
it's a wonder the doors didn't fall off.
We'd crash and splash into the cool water,
ignoring the sound of the whitecaps
as they chopped off the tops of waves.
Tripping over each other, we'd laugh
as our white bellies no longer confined
by a steamy hot car would
feel the coolness trickle over us
like a brook over the once dusty stones.
Then our honey-coloured bodies would pop
up like firecrackers, over the sand dunes,
tumbling and stumbling into somersaults,
rolling down the hill as if it were snow covered.
So light and small, we were like paper bags
twisting in the wind.
And we'd climb back up the hill.
never tiring to do it over and over again
all summer.

In Hiding

It happened as fast as a snapshot.
She was gone.
Jessie had run away
because for her
it was a day of mourning.
It was Mama's wedding day
when she'd marry that man.
Mama sent me to fetch her
because she knew I'd know
where Jessie would be hiding
And she was right.
I saw her in the distance.
I readied my camera
the way a soldier would ready his gun.
Jessie stood triumphant, defiant even,
on top of the train, the great iron horse
as though she was determined
to never come home.
I remember
as soon as I took her picture
she collapsed into tears
And I had to steady her,
help her get down safely.
I hid my face in her little yellow dress
because I didn't want Mama
to marry that man either.

Falling in Love

Sitting on a big, slippery red balloon
I have no control over its direction.
Higher and higher I go.
As I look down
my world gets smaller
I should have got off a long time ago
The drop is getting worse and worse
Either I'm going to slip off this thing
Or I'll end up in the branch of a tree
Which undoubtedly will burst the whole thing
What I fear most is that I'll
keep on going up and up
Until I can't see anyone any more
And have to live on a far-off planet alone.

Snow

"So what is snow like?"
asked the Cuban.
The child beside her
looked up as I responded.
"Imagine those clouds
are huge eiderdown pillows
that burst open
and small fragments of
feathers toss and turn
in their bright whiteness
until they touch the ground
ever so lightly creating
the illusion of sugar covering
the earth."

Endless Reflections

Does art reflect life
or life reflect art?
In the sky's blackness are
tiny shimmering candles.
Inside the cabin stars
are burning in small glasses.
Inside me I'm
glowing with warmth.
Outside I'm grateful
to be surrounded by friends.
Does life reflect art?
Or does art reflect life?

The Challenge

There he was
A small thumbnail of a toad
Always out of his civvies
In his camouflaged uniform
Well-equipped by nature
To be protected
From any predator
Motionless among the
Crumpled dead leaves
He sat as if he were a pebble
I'd make a game of waiting
I'd outwait this toad
I'd stand motionless
Until he moved
I'd prove that the rush
Of the city hadn't created
An impatience within me
Standing still in the afternoon sun
The sun's heat burned
The back of my neck
I stared at the toad
While he stared at me
I began to think
of the lake's cool retreat
of how lovely a sandwich would taste
of how pleasant sitting is
of how much time had passed
of how stubborn this toad was
of how much I hated this game
I was probably there
for the same time that
it took you to read this poem.
I turned and walked away.

Our Fearless Men

They craved adventure.
After all, it was advertised
in the travel brochure.
So despite the Cubans'
caution not to enter the angry sea,
they hoisted their sea kayaks
on their city-strained backs
and lowered them to the rough waters.
Their mission accepted
to rescue their "machismo."
They frantically paddled against the current
until they reached the booming six foot waves.
Bill, though usually a strong seaman
was unable to hold back the tidal wave motion,
water rushing into his kayak
like a raging beast.
It fiercely slapped his kayak
on its backside.
But Tai, only an arm's length away
grabbed his comrade
as he took the plunge
into the ocean's depths
and pulled him out by the hair
(Or maybe it was his arm).
It's all a little sketchy
as we savour this souvenir story
sitting by the fire in Canada's
cabin in winter.

"... Who Stretchest
Out the Heavens Like a Curtain."
Ps. 104: 2

Each day the curtain opens to the Cuban sky
with burning red flaming colour
shifting to tangerine orange
awakening to faded amarillo
until the clouds take centre stage
moving sluggishly in shapes
like boats sailing towards the horizon.
We lie on the beach, book in hand,
living in the fanciful world of fiction
awaiting the curtain of darkness
to bring a close to our vacation.

Cuba in a Snapshot

Under the shade of the Cuban palms
one man busily cuts and clips the hair
of a man who already has short hair.
Another man, with pants too baggy big, paces
forwards and backwards as he talks.
A fourth man sits on a stump listening.
Faces full of expression as they exchange words.
I watch from the bus.
To me, they are talking about the revolution.
To another onlooker they might be talking of
a miserable life in Santiago de Cuba.
To me, they are passionate about life.
To another, they might think they wish
for modern material luxuries.
To me, they are being saved from endless hours,
hypnotized by the waves of the boob tube.
To another they are deprived of freedom's blessings.
To me, they are experiencing friendship
In a way most people don't understand.

Cabin Healing

As many candles alight in our cabin
as in a Catholic church
with a similar reverence
in this forest stillness.
The fire sings a soft hissing song
void of lyrics.

The scent of cedar burning seeps
through evergreen branches.
The small genies leave our coffee cups
as you and I, like scribes, busily write
poetry at the picnic table.

Home

I used to think that home [my consciousness]
was a place where I was comfortable,
where the gooseberry shutters
wouldn't keep me silent,
where the door bell
alerted me to learn more,
where the windows helped me
see others from a distance,
where my door remained locked,
my ideas safely secure.
Then the Holocaust survivors
invited me into their homes.
We sat on their summer porches,
swinging freely on the veranda,
feeling the breeze buzzing through trees
while the lemonade sloshed
between the ice cubes.
They guided me through memories
of family members who were
suffocated, gassed or starved to death.
In their homes there was no bitter hatred
That doormat had been wiped clean
"Hatred only hurts the one who hates," one said.
The Nazis took their houses, jewels, clothes,
even their loved ones.
But they could never take their homes
Their pride, confidence and self-worth.

"Now I Lay me Down to Sleep"

Childhood words that
repeat like waves in the lake.
As I lie in this hard wooden pew
a cold, drafty wooden boat
rocking back and forth, I drift,
always drifting, never on solid ground.
A moment of calm breezes over me
as I lie still in this open casket
to dream my last dream,
a stowaway hiding from the world
lost in this haven of God
where people come in close communion.
But where I, alone, notice
candles of hope snuffed out,
guilt seeping into my bones
with the dank air in this church
embraced by a pungent smell of mildew
of things past, not present.
Even now, I know my visit is not to pray
but for the hope of warmth.
I try hard not to fall asleep
but like all my sins, I can't resist.
"If I should die before I wake
I pray the Lord, (that there is a) soul to take."
And high above me is a great light
beaming through the stained glass.
Above the confessional box
shines a rainbow of words on the wall
"Behold, my beloved son.
With whom I am well pleased."

September 11, 2001

News that won't fade
Her words linger in thought
"Thank goodness, the towers
came to their knees
crumbling within themselves.
Imagine if, falling like trees
the 1300 foot tall giants
had fallen into all of Manhattan."
Perhaps it soothes the suffering.

Stop the Free Fall

On September 11, as television
etched into our memories
the image of two planes
knifing the trade towers,
I found my thought go into free fall.
The planes were missiles in the mind
imploding ideas of hostility and hatred;
I didn't even know for whom.
The aggressive antagonism I felt
was quickly heading me for
Ground Zero.
I had to stop the free fall,
ease up on the throttle of thought,
take control of my thinking,
use any energy to reclaim a sense of peace,
take my pulse off the panic button,
reflect on life in its eternal nature,
take moments in the day
to find my equilibrium.
And navigate my thoughts back to God.

Last Summer

Do you remember?
Last summer
lying here on life's shore
coolness shifting under our bodies
with each sandy grain
like salt running through an hour glass
memories sifting
through our fingers and toes
were alive in the darkness.
Lady Di and Mother Theresa were gone
and with them
went some of the earth's kindness,
squeezed, or maybe wrenched,
from this dark earthy hole.
There was uncertainty in the air.
The rich, navy-coloured sky
was like a thick, dark quilt
clouds rolled with curves and turns like
bumps of a bed made in haste,
stretched in the stillness
we pondered our existence.

Flying High

Flying makes me courageous.
I figure it's as close to skydiving
as I'm ever going to get.
It's an inspiration.
As I climb above the grey clouds,
(that look dirty, like old slush
from stale snow)
I forget my troubles and worries
because at 20,000 feet,
they all seem so small, so insignificant.
Flying forces me to attempt
to express the thrill of drifting
among the white mounds of comfort
that look like white deserts of snow
primed for a game of fox and geese
that transform into gauzy patches with tears
that I begin to see through.
Far below me are computer boards,
solid green with little circuit clusters of houses
and brownish patches of farmer's fields.
I take a moment to be in awe
of a technology that is greater than man.

Spider Spinners

In the stillness of early morn
We wander
Tear drops on green beefy blades
Spotlights of sun stretch through
slender snake-like trees
Kaleidoscoping light flickers
Casting moving shadows through the light
On ferns and spring foliage
Soft trickling water sends a cedar scent to air
Glistening jewel-like patterns among the branches
Fragile, gently crafted webs of silk
By spinners proudly suspended in mid-circle
Trapeze artists from birth
Showing off their talent
In their airy studio galleries.

The City of Toronto

Where was I when it grew up?
The slender, graceful buildings
Now multiplied into mega monsters
Skyscrapers with steel skin
Jewelled with glitzy lights
Without history or reverence
Replacing the lush green pastures
Of a time vanished forever.

Rain Dance

she was a mother
like no other
she loved to share
with her girls
the great simplicity of life
so when it rained one afternoon
and frowns appeared on the faces
of her little darlings,
Diane embraced her daughters
took one under each arm
as they were small enough to carry
she swirled and twirled them
in the backyard and then taught them
to skip, jump and dance with the raindrops
occasionally opening their mouths
to drink in the tears of joy from the heavens

Ever with me

When you build...
Your ability and agility
Are in your strength and skill
To complete any task

When you sing...
You are my unsung hero
A voice unrecognized
In beauty, talent and might
Whether with hymns in church
Or roaring solos in the shower

When you photograph...
You share your vision
I know what joy you add
And what sorrows you take out
Of my life

When you write...
You embed with elastic humour
Your genius in choice of word
Your letter poems tell me
Your thoughts and emotions

So that when you laugh...
Whether it be at movies, TV or our own jokes
You include me in your comfort
We smile together

When you cry...
I shed your tears
I know your disappointment
I feel your pain.

So that even when...
You have to go miles away
We are always a part of each other
You are ever with me, my love.

Haiku for my husband

Most men sleep with women
My husband sleeps with earplugs

Cuba

Is it the beauty of the countryside?
The spider-top palms, nature's fireworks
exploding everywhere in the landscape?
Or the rugged faces turning to sweet smiles?
Or maybe it is knowing that the sun is still alive?
No, it is the kindness
of the Cubans that calls me to return.

The Mist

The mist hovers over the lake
Weighing heavier with its thickness
Leaving behind an offering,
A comforting quilt of smoke
Over past agonies, past wounds, past scars,
Seeping into the harsh lines
Scraping out the
Cruel childhood memories,
Left in rocks at
The altar of Lake Memphremagog.

Purdy Country

In a foreground of purple hills
lies country that calms unsettled spirits.

Great white swans, soaring goddesses
flap their wings stridently, making
whirring sounds like a child's over-wound toy
released into open, endless heavens.

Marshlands edge into skies,
covering an aquatic underworld
while a back-wood's scent of cedars seeps
into air, mingling like campfire smoke.

Roads spill up and down as
rollercoasters, offering glimpses
of farms divided into caramel squares,
and distant aqua-blue waters

Beyond mustard tamaracks,
but not beyond imagination.

Defending its Turf

The day I saw a white swan
chasing a Canada Goose
through the march
into full flight
I knew my instinct
had been correct.
As beautiful as they are,
there have been far too many
Canada Geese in the city.
As politically incorrect
as it might be
I was delighted to see,
in the country,
nature was defending its turf
and pushing back a bit.

Selected Prose
by Kimberley Grove

I am honoured to present in this section selected prose written by Kim during a remarkably extended period of time. Kim found time—and had the gift—for writing plenty of material that covered poetry that we enjoyed in the previous section, plus stories, newspaper articles, chronicles, interviews, reflections, personal experiences and thoughts she shared, etc. She ably navigated different functional styles. From them I chose these.

Thus, we have the privilege of collecting into a single volume much of her oeuvre. Kim wrote poetry to allow serene moments to linger. She enjoyed the exchange with other writers who encouraged her to express her individuality. Her prose was published in The Christian Science Monitor, The Boston Globe, The Toronto Star and The Globe and Mail and many other periodicals.

Having left the city a few years ago

Having left the city a few years ago, I thought it might help to reminisce on the "better" aspects of the "better way" to travel. Riding the transit rails at rush hour is like being thrust into an "Outward Bound" exercise every day. Some people pay big bucks to put their body through the rigours of such exercises. In comparison, the Toronto Transit offers it for less than a cup of Starbucks' coffee. I usually started my excursion at busy Bloor and Yonge, an overly popular station. Sometimes I wondered if the entire city of Toronto was not sharing the thrill.

The eerie sound along the tracks that shrilled to the pitch of a squealing wild boar could be frightening if you didn't know it was the train approaching. When the train glided into sight so full of people that some bodies were pressed against the doors like catfish clinging to their fish tank, I would start to feel my temperature rise. There was always the temptation to give up and go home at that moment.

I was only occasionally pleasantly surprised when the doors opened and released a flood of unfamiliar faces. I always stepped aside. The tidal wave of suits, sweaters or shirts that stampeded towards me were also a little frightening, but that's the name of the game. It's as if these excruciating exercises are aimed at testing a person's sensibilities. People discover their potential to stay calm in cramped, crowded conditions.

If I managed to get into the train on my first try, I would dart for the center pole. Much like rock climbing, I would try to hold on to the pole tightly, knowing that the consequences of letting go were disastrous. I was never quite ready to just throw myself into the experience. I guess I am classified as the non-aggressive, introverted type.

There was no point in even thinking of looking for a vacant seat. Those had disappeared at stations much earlier in the hinterlands, on the outskirts of the city centre.

One time I had no choice but to fling myself into the black void, the spot in the middle of the crowd where there is nothing to hold on to. There I experienced something like bumper cars, without the cars, bodies banging against each other uncontrollably. I've heard this part of the adventure described by others as a similar sensation to going through the hot cycle in your dryer.

It is also a test of a person's balance. I didn't always score big in this area. I remember reaching out to get help from the man who was wrapped around centre pole while absorbed in his book. I guess he forgot to read the portion of the manual that talked about the value of teamwork on these excursions. He let me fall back onto the man sitting listening to tunes on his ipod. I wasn't particularly popular on that excursion. I don't remember making any new friends, but the experience was successful in testing my personal limits.

There was also the time in high school that I tested everyone else's personal limits when I took my putt on the TTC. I had taken it home for the weekend to practice for my shot putt event the following week. I was carrying too many books in my arms. I dropped the 16 lb putt, just missing a woman's foot. She smiled until she tried to pick up. Probably she thought it was a baseball. That day I did find a seat as far away from everyone as I could.

The truly best part of this "TTC The Better Way" was how much it helped my job. After traveling through the wilderness, alone among strangers, I would always appreciate work so much more when I finally got there. It was as if I'd reached my goal. I was ready to brave any new business battles.

After years of traveling on the transit, I finally decided that I'd learned as much as I was ever going to learn from these "Outward Bound" experiences. My husband and I moved to the country to join the rest of Canada, living without the crowded luxury of the, so called, lovely TTC.

Brighton Streets

Young Street stood out to me right away when we moved to Brighton. Finally, some people who can spell. Not like those crazy Torontonians who came up with Yonge Street. And the people here didn't seem all hung up on their road being the longest street the North America or Canada. In fact, it is such a short street that it changes its name halfway through town and becomes Prince Edward.

This all led me to wondering how many of the streets in Brighton got their names.

Main Street is fairly obvious. Some no-nonsense person said this is the main street in town so that's what we'll call it. Maybe someone else joined in and called one if its tributaries Young Street as it was not an old street.

Then, of course, there are those people who are always finding ways to have their names on things like plaques, pews and benches. Thus we have Percy and Ross Rd. I wonder if these were the same people who earlier in life carved their names into trees, or wet cement. It occurred to me that there are whole families that think this way. Thus we get Ferguson Hill and Simpson Street.

Back in the old days, there were probably those who called streets after their hometown and so we get Old York Street. Or maybe those who came from the old country, thus Bonn Street.

Naturally, when they came they were struck by all the beautiful tress so we get names like Evergreen lane, Elm Street, Sumach lane and for those who knew nothing about nature Wood Street.

I guess when you're first trying to come up with the names for roads in a new community the bureaucrats, not wanting to show any favoritism, would call them names like County Road number 24, or Brighton-Cramhe Boundary Road. I wonder how many fights there were about the name Brighton coming first on that one. It is awfully close to Huff Road which might give some indication.

Then I can imagine in later years that a woman in the municipal office insisting on some streets being named after women, thus we have Allison, Elizabeth and Hazel. It might sound sexist but I imagine she also named Darling Road. Perhaps she had a poetic flair and referred to Windy Lane which cannot be straight. Telephone Road might have been called that because the trees along it looked like telephone poles or it is the street where they put in the first telephone.

You get a feel for Brighton's history with Calf Pasture and Fish Hatchery Roads.

Before you become too alarmed, this is all speculation. I don't really know how streets are named. When I lived in Toronto I guess I always thought it was one person rather than a committee that did the naming. Otherwise, how many people would call a street Avenue Road?

Of course, this brings up another question, how do they decide whether to call a street a road, avenue or drive? But that is a topic for a whole different article.

The Menorca Story

I sat on the cold kitchen floor in my pajamas, waiting for my friend's phone call. The black wall telephone above was like a guillotine and when the phone rang my life would change forever. Annie had called from Barcelona, Spain, the week before asking me if I wanted to share an apartment near the Ramblas de Catalunya while teaching English to Spaniards. My lack of a teaching degree or inability to speak Spanish hadn't deterred her. "It doesn't matter. You have a university degree and English is your first language. That's all the school needs." I had no excuse. I knew that if I turned down this opportunity to learn about another part of the world, I would regret it for the rest of my life.

We referred to those times as our "Hemingway days." I was able to survive on 12 hours of teaching a week. Our apartment was full of life. The Catalan woman, Adelaide, that we rented from had a great admiration for English. She and I would sit reading Shakespeare together in the living room and she would shake her blonde hair and gasp at some of new meaning she had acquired of words like "star-crossed lovers" or And I would get a new appreciation for these plays as if I had the pleasure of reading them for the first time. But a challenge I had was in learning Spanish (Castellano). Adelaide's brother had been imprisoned during Franco's time for waving the Catalan flag so she forbid Spanish to be spoken in the home. I had the option of Catalan or English. So this made it awkward to communicate sometimes. Consequently, when one day her Catalan boyfriend called to ask where she was I struggled to explain her whereabouts. "She is waiting for a man on the street," I explained, which only caused a long pause and then a chuckle. On another occasion I was at a large dinner party I did what I was in the habit of doing and just gave a Spanish pronunciation to an English word and hoped that I would be understood, so I said to the woman sitting beside me, "Estoy embarasado," which I thought would get across the fact that "I'm embarrassed," as I didn't know much Spanish. The conversation at the dinner party stopped. Everyone stared at me. Finally, Annie helped, "You just said that you are pregnant." We all laughed uncontrollably.

We also shared the apartment with an American actress who had Lucille Ball red hair and quite the actor's life. She had the largest bedroom in the apartment that faced out to the street. She slept all day and was on stage at night so the only time I would see her would be during the day when I would be running out to teach a class. She would be wandering the halls in her long silk nightgown hoping to find some leftovers from Adelaida's gourmet cooking. There was no fridge in the kitchen so we had to resort to hanging our milk and butter in a bag out the window, hoping that the string wouldn't break. It also meant going to market everyday. I had a terrible time getting used to the price of vegetables according to their kilogram weight. One day I returned with a huge bag of green peppers and the next with only two potatoes.

Of my teaching days one experience stands out more than any other. When I look back on my behaviour I define it as cultural anxiety or new relationship jitters, some would say I was simply a bit neurotic. I had a class scheduled at my apartment in the late afternoon before meeting up with a new boyfriend, Tony. We were scheduled to take off to the small island of Menorca, in the southern seas but I was somewhat apprehensive about the arrangements. I had been feeling slightly uncomfortable about the new relationship. The trip was planned with Tony and his sister, Alex, who I didn't know very well. I tried my best to hide my apprehensive feelings but I'm afraid I didn't succeed very well and in the hours before I left I was wondering what on earth I was doing. My apartment was a reflection of my thinking – it was a mess.

Antonio, Maria and Jesus arrived promptly as usual. Their goal was learning English before they took a trip to America. I tried my best to hide the chaos in my apartment. They either didn't mind or didn't notice. They were keen students and it wasn't hard to get them engaged in learning but suddenly there was a blackout – No Lights. I looked down at my papers. I have to admit that the lesson had not been prepared in much detail before the class, so to find myself suddenly in the dark was true in more ways than one. Strangely enough it never occurred to me to have the students go home. We had been discussing the parts of the house; door, window, table, chair, etc so at that moment I began pointing at items and presenting English words. In hind sight I suppose I was excited about the trip and was subconsciously wondering how I would finish packing without lights.

The next half hour was a little wild. I was probably concerned about filling the next half hour in the dark. I pointed to the pitcher in the cabinet, I remembered that my mother had always corrected me on the proper pronunciation of the words pitcher and picture. It was a complete association of words in a situation like this and so I began to explain that picture and pitcher were two different things and should be pronounced differently. From there I began to explain that the pitcher you put water in is the same word as the pitcher in baseball and that's where the fun really began. I got totally side tracked by desperately trying to explain the game baseball, I explained by running around the tiny space between our living room and an imaginary home plate which brought us back to the plate in the cabinet and I stopped running. I sat down calmly and pointed to the plate and the bowl.

Thank heavens they asked about tennis. (I'm only surprised I didn't stand up on tiptoe crying "Anyone for tennis?) I explained the racket, the ball and the court. Tennis being a rather simple game, it didn't take much explanation, but I found they wanted to know the name of some parts of the court. I tried to explain that it had been a long time since I'd played tennis. Even then it had only been casually volleying the ball back and forth, so I explained I was not much of a tennis player and didn't remember the names of the parts of the court but Maria insisted on persisting. I had to bear with her as she explained that in Spanish it was "malla" which didn't mean a thing to me. Then she said something about "pescado," fish which just confused me even more, and then I remembered the word "Luv" they used in English. "Oh" I said and began to explain the scoring system and this confused them even more. The word Luv seemed to please Antonio. Except I couldn't remember when we used the word "Luv" and it was not the word Love although I did remember the scoring started at 15. I loved Maria but she was still preoccupied with the court and busily drew a bad map of a tennis court without the assistance of any light.

However the light did dawn when I saw her picture not pitcher. (Back to the beginning of this whole riddle). It was the word "net" that she was looking for. Of course, the ball goes over the fish net. Well, by that time the lesson hour was over thank goodness. They seemed as eager to leave as I was to see the back of them. I finished the lesson by using the word "door" – don't let the door hit you on your way out.

The Magic of Philip Sun

If you think magic is confined to kids, then you must have missed Philip Sun's photographic presentation on Tuesday, May 6. Sun spoke to an audience of approximately fifty adults (standing room only to latecomers). Before their eyes he changed ordinary snap shots into fine photographic works of art with the aid of Photoshop and a big screen projector.

Philip Sun has been competing in photography contests for ten years after co-owning a camera store in Toronto since 1979. He is ranked seventh in the world's top ten exhibitors in The Photographic Society of America's Who's Who.

The Digital Photography special interest group, a branch of the Computer Club, invited Sun to perform a titanic task. They sent Sun samples of their photographs (over 100) and asked him to show how they could be improved.

Sun performed his magic. Unlike some masters, he was willing to share his tricks. Step by step on the big screen, he showed how best to enhance images. His first trick could have been called the "ugly duckling." He transformed a greyish image of a swan and goslings into a jewel-beaked wonder, the focus of the image. The awes and oohs of the audience were as if he had pulled a rabbit out of a hat.

His next trick was to show how cutting out elements in the picture removes optical obstructions to the viewer. "Now you see, it now you don't," he said cropping out a sky in one image and taking out a branch in another. He tweaked exposure to give more depth, enhanced colour, emphasized shadow and light, making dark areas crisp and bright areas stand out.

"If you like the psychedelic Pink Floyd stuff, you're going to like this picture. If not, bear with me," said Sun. He took the image of a church's interior, turned it inside out so that the end result was an abstract of intricate shapes.

He also showed how to superimpose one picture over another creating a nostalgic mood. Layering the face of an elderly woman over the image of a castle, he used the detail of the rock to emphasize the aged face. This demonstrated that it is the creativity of the artist, as well as the thrill of all Photoshop's magic wands that leave the viewer looking at a masterpiece. To highlight the quality of the image, Sun created a border around each photo, giving the impression of the new art work hanging on a wall.

The entertaining performance was a success. Sun had made the whole process appear effortless. Bruce Tollefson, one of the conveners of the digital group enjoyed what he saw. "Philip shows how simple it is to take an ordinary photo and make it striking."

The Griffin Poetry Prize 2004

On Wednesday, June 2, the Cinderella story came to life for the Canadian poetry scene. Instead of the usual small gathering of 20-30 committed poetry fans, the large auditorium at the Edward Johnson building was filled.

The Griffin awards established by the prince of poetry, Scott Griffin, honoured four international and three Canadian poets by asking this shortlist to read from their works. Each read eloquently in their unique style.

It couldn't have been an easy choice for the judges (Billy Collins, Bill Manhire and Phyllis Webb) to pick two winners. Anne Simpson's gentle words in sentences like "Only this: one hand over another, our hearts folded like wings, sleep," brought a calmness and peace to the listener. (We learned the next day that she won the Canadian award. The international winner, August Kleinzahler's poems flowed like music, each word a note each sentence full of rhythm.)

There were special moments. Leslie Greentree, in particular, made the audience feel at ease when she expressed the thrill of being on stage with such amazing writers.

We heard the greatness. We crowded around the poets being honoured and let the literary icons like Margaret Atwood and Michael Ondaatje have their peace. With their fellow trustees of the awards Robert Robertson, David Young and Robert Hass they were there to pay tribute to these poets rather, than be honoured themselves.

Probably what impressed me as much as the poetry was the humility of the poets. When we timidly approached them for autographs, one seemed so unsure of his talent asking us if he had read all right. We assured him he had.

I get excited at such events; I blurted out to David Kirby that he had my vote. He replied, "it's your vote (as a reader) that counts." And I think that is how the audience felt like it counted that we were there. We felt like we were at a royal ball, honoured to learn more about this wonderful art form. I felt like the Rotarian in David Kirby's poem.

" ...I get up to read my poetry,
and when I'm finished, one Rotarian expresses
understandable confusion at exactly what it is
I'm doing and wants to know what poetry is, exactly,
so I tell him that when most nonpoets think
of the word "poetry," they think of "lyric poetry,"
not "narrative poetry," whereas what I'm doing
Is "narrative poetry" of the kind performed
by, not that I am in any way comparing myself
to them, Homer, Dante and Milton,
and he's liking this, he's smiling and nodding,"
and when I finish my little speech,
he shouts, "Thank you, Doctor! Thank you
for educating us!"

(*The Griffin Poetry Prize of $40,000 to each winner is the most prestigious poetry prize awarded in Canada*).

Making history come alive:
An interview with author Morgan Wade

"Put down that book. It's time for supper." Morgan wanted to obey his mother, but the lion Aslan was in a horrific battle with the White Witch so he couldn't think of eating.

This might have been Morgan Wade's childhood scenario because he loved the CS Lewis series of Narnia books when he was a boy. They ignited his imagination. He told his parents that he was going to be an author when he grew up. Living in the small town of Tottenham helped with that dream as he had his favourite teacher, David Anderson, for grades 3, 5 and 6. "He gave us many creative writing projects," said Wade.

Wade lives in Kingston now, a city steeped in history, with constant visual reminders of it in relics like Fort Henry. He decided to do an in-depth study of its history. "There has been a lot of history written about Kingston. It lends itself to storytelling so well. It just cries out for novels."

The power of fiction is that from the safety of one's own couch, a person can really go deeply into the story and ask oneself important questions. When Wade reads he can't help but wonder what the historical figures were thinking. Were they afraid, motivated by conscience to do the right thing, or concerned about patriotism? He imagines their emotions that led them to their actions. It is that questioning that leads to interesting characters for his novels.

Each of his books begin with an in-depth look at history of a specific period. "I hope they [the readers] enjoy it, I hope it is entertaining but for someone who loves history I hope that it transports them to a different time and place and they get the chance to inhabit the lives of some of the characters, to imagine what it was like to be these people."

He expects the reader to examine their own life and wonder what they would do if they had been in a given situation.

George Orwell, author of Animal Farm and Nineteen Eighty-four, is Wade's favourite author. Wade thinks he has read everything he wrote. His most admired work is Orwell's essay Politics in the English language. To him, it shows that "Clear prose can help you fight dictatorships and wrong thinking, help you identify truth from fiction. He [Orwell] was a champion of human freedom and dignity in the face of huge institutional challenges."

If the reader thinks of Orwell's essay Why I Write, looking at the four points he makes it is clear that Wade is incorporating some of the same principles.

1) Sheer egoism: Desire to seem clever, to be talked about, to be remembered after death, to get your own back on grown-ups who snubbed you in childhood, etc. Egoism is not to be confused with egotism as Wade is a humble writer. Enjoying his clear writing style, he was asked if he would accept a writers-in-residence position. He modestly answered, "I don't think I have the profile. I think it would be valuable work. Editing for me, clarifies my own writing." He remembers telling a neighbour that he hoped to be a writer, but the response was not encouraging. "She took the wind out of my sails by saying that I shouldn't bother because they are a dime a dozen." Though Wade has a memory of that comment, it didn't stop him. He studied at the Humber School of Writing where he learned the importance of being ruthless when editing. He is the author of three novels, The Last Stoic, Bottles and Glass and Paper & Rags, published by Hidden Brook Press.

2) Aesthetic enthusiasm: Perception of beauty in the external world, or on the other hand, in words and their right arrangement. "Good prose is like a window pane," wrote George Orwell. Wade has adopted the concept in his writing. His description is that window to the external world at times and his choice of words is the right arrangement as in this passage of The Last Stoic.

"The sun's leading edge dipped behind the low hills ahead and shadows distorted the landscape. Marcus refastened the broach of his tunic against the cooling air. The monotony of the journey had inflamed his imagination and he was aware for the first time of his remoteness from home. A misshapen shrub around the bend resembled, for a moment, a prowling animal. Rustling in the long grasses betrayed sneaking highwaymen.

He crested a slope. Every three hundred feet or so, on either side of the road for as far as he could see, stood crucifixes, one after another, silhouetted black and looming against the reddening sky, with a slumping figure fastened to each one." (The Last Stoic, page 10)

He avoids the clichés. There are no honey melting sunsets, and yet the reader can imagine the scene.

Another example of this vivid writing is when he switches to modern day America and writes, "Mark had camped down at a rest-stop along a stretch of the freeway where the Interstate became the New Jersey turnpike, just past the many rows of hulking 18-wheeler rigs, orange and red running lights like patio lanterns strung along the perimeters of their cargo, idling diesel engines emitting an endless hushed rattle, drivers catatonic in the fold-out bunks of their compact cabs.

A quarter mile away the turnpike roared with a host of travelers finding their way through the darkness. The windscreen glowed softly with the unremitting white lights of the distant sixteen pump service station. Inside the car, dashboard instruments cast a low, blue phosphorescence. He sipped from a can of frigid, metallic-tasting Budweiser. For a moment, he felt intrepid. A stranger amongst strangers. Unburdened." (The Last Stoic, page 17)

In Wade's second novel, Bottles and Glass, he takes the reader into the taverns of old Kingston after the war of 1812. His writing was so genuine to the period that in 2016 a talented theatre director, Brett Christopher (now managing and artistic director of The 1000 Islands Playhouse), in Kingston requested Wade to convert his novel to a play. It was sold out for 5 nights.

As the events in the book took place in the taverns of old Kingston, the play was extended by having the audience visit bars in the city with the actors. "It was a thrill of a life time," said Wade, "to see the characters you have written come to life."

3) Historical impulse: Desire to see things as they are, to find out true facts and store them up for the use of posterity.

Certainly, there is an historical impulse in all of Wade's novels. Too often students have found Canadian history lacking in excitement. By detailing the challenges of characters in various classes in the 1800s, he helps the reader realize what society was like in those times. In that time period, Canada offered an immigrant the chance at starting life again as one character comes from England to escape a scandal, the protagonist is constantly struggling to make a fair wage and a woman is saved from prostitution by becoming a doctor's assistant.

Wade brings out the plight of women in those times, as well as the poverty that was rampant To bring history to life as Wade endeavours to do, demands a great deal of research. Words like grape shot (ammunition for gun or cannon), or quills (pens for writing) or pelisse (a woman's cloak) all help to authenticate the history he is writing about. An example of how he crafts them into his story is in this sample:

"Jeremy laid the quill he had borrowed from Antoine into the narrow trough of the writing box. He dusted a measure of fine pounce over the still damp words, gently vibrated the sheet of paper, and then tipped it, allowing the excess powdered bone to fall to the floor. Once the ink was dry, he folded the letter and sealed it with melted beeswax from the lit candle on the writing desk." (Paper and Rags, Page 224)

One of his characters, Lilac, is shamed as a prostitute and displayed for the towns people to gawk at in the pillory before being sent to jail. His portrayal of her encourages the reader's compassion, rather than disdain.

4) Political purpose: using the word 'political' in the widest possible sense. Desire to push the world in a certain direction, to alter other people's idea of the kind of society that they should strive after.

Wade's book, "The Last Stoic," is a reflection of this idea as his hope is that his reader will see the parallel of Ancient Rome and modern United States. He read a lot about stoicism. He comments that stoicism "seemed to be a fiber that made ancient Rome, when it was great, strong." He fears that the stoicism of the original founders of the US has been lost to the detriment of the country and the world. As Orwell states, "I write it [the book] because there is some lie that I want to expose, some fact to which I want to draw attention, and my initial concern is to get a hearing." Wade has the reader's attention by comparing the two societies.

When the hero of the Ancient Roman story, Marcus, meets an old man in prison he comments on what is happening in Rome. The reader can't help but think of today's society. "Two primary passions afflict us Marcus, Romans no less than any others.

Appetite and fear. They are excessive impulses. Disobedient to reason. Ruled by these passions people become slaves to pleasure or distress. It's the easiest thing to do; the passions are always there, beckoning. They can be held in check, but never can be eliminated. It takes a lifetime of study, training, and selfdiscipline to rule oneself." (The Last Stoic, page 217)

Wade's process for writing is to begin with an overarching concept, sketch out an outline and then fill in the detail. As his books are historical, he does research and then he starts to put plot points down. "With Paper and Rags, I had that last scene in mind and I knew I wanted to get there." He was able to do that in less than the 9 drafts it took on The Last Stoic. "

One area that Wade might differ from Orwell is he sees writing as more pleasure than drudgery whereas Orwell said, "Writing a book is a horrible, exhausting struggle, like a long bout of some painful illness."

While Orwell spoke of why he wrote, Wade encourages others to write. He has five points for the wannabe writer.

1) Find books on writing to see how others do it. Two suggestions are Bird by Bird by Anne Lamott and Writing fiction: a guide to narrative craft by Janet Burroway.

2) "Share your work with people you trust who will give you substantial, honest feedback. If you can find somebody like that, that's a real treasure. Friends and family will willingly read your stuff but they probably won't give you complete honesty and you really need that."

3) "Be willing to read others' work and give in-depth feedback for them will always improve your own writing because you will be focusing on what works and what doesn't work."

4) Even with a day job, it's still important to put aside specific writing time. (Wade has organized his work schedule so Fridays are his writing days.)

5) "Write and read as much as you can." And Wade follows his own advice. He has become so attached to his character, Jeremy Castor, that he plans to write another book that focuses on Jeremy's life and times, and, of course, the setting will be Kingston.

A Different Havana Vacation

Attending the play "Leo" the night before flying to Havana, in Cuba's current political climate, could be deemed equivalent to going to see the movie the Titanic before departing on a cruise.

"Leo" is all about a tumultuous time in Chile's past where it wasn't uncommon for people to go missing after Augusto Pinochet overthrew Allende's socialist government.

There is currently a lot of speculation on what will happen to Cuba when its leader, Fidel Castro, passes on. Knowing that recently Castro has been struggling to keep his place on this earth, I didn't want to be faced with a situation similar to that of Chile in which a violent uprising ended in panic and chaos. I didn't want to be a disappearing person. This was to be a vacation, a time to relax in the sun, away from stress, not a time that I wanted to be seen by my family on the 11:00 news and not seen again.

My husband, on the other hand, is more adventuresome, always looking for the opportunity to be a part of a special historic moment.

For one thing, he had done the unusual by organizing a vacation with 10 people, 6 of them strangers. As president of the Canada Cuba Literary Alliance, he had coordinated poetry readings for Canadian poets, at the Havana university, the central library, our hotel and a final televised reading at the International Book Festival. Of course, they do things a little differently in Cuba so we had no idea if any of the events would happen, until we got there. In typically unpredictable Cuban time, the last event meant sitting outside the Book Institute for a day waiting to speak to the director to confirm that everything was in place.

There were times that I felt like I was living an episode of Gilligan's Island. These five Canadian poets and their family or friends were similar to the characters you might find stranded on a deserted island.

John B. Lee, the poet laureate from Brantford, was like the professor, so well-read that it was a waste of my time to even break the spine of the book I brought. His wife and I listened to him share his observations about life. "Have you ever noticed that nightly news is sponsored by constipation, stomach and headache drugs? I've come to the conclusion that the nightly news is not good for you," he said.

The Ginger character, Linda Rogers from Victoria, B.C. was the most celebrated celebrity among us, having published several books. She had ever-ready energy. If it hadn't been for a recovering sprained ankle, she probably would have invited Castro to go dancing. She brought her granddaughter of 13, Sophie, who once she overcame initial shyness had no problem asking the direct questions. "If you're married, why isn't your wife on this trip?" she asked Doug, the past editor of Poetry Canada.

Graham Ducker, a former kindergarten teacher, was like Mr. Howe. He and his wife Stella (aka Mrs. Howe) had never traveled outside North America. A vacation to them was baking on a beach in Florida. They immediately changed their hotel room to the ocean side. Stella didn't leave the room the first day. They seemed to attract problems. Their new room sprang a leak; their floor was flooded.

My British writing friend, Susan, was similar to Marianne in her enthusiastic efforts to speak Spanish and commune with the natives. She and Doug journeyed off to a part of Havana few tourists tread. They almost had their cameras confiscated.

My husband, Skipper, was relentless at making sure everyone was at the right place at the right time. The finale of the International Book Festival was overwhelming as the crowds were comparable to Toronto's Word on the Street event. I learned quickly that Cubans love books as much as they do music.

Like Gilligan, I was a little nervous much of the time. Usually, I was able to put aside any fears of disappearing people until the day my husband didn't show for the bus back to the hotel.

I looked from my watch to the long stretch of sea walkway, called the Malecon. There was no sign of him. Everyone was ready to board the bus. "Where is he?" Everyone kept asking. The only thing I knew was that the last time I saw him was in the marketplace.

Finally, my inner panic was pacified. Among the three musicians that were meandering along the Malecon was an overly-enthusiastic drummer. My husband had bought a drum at the market. I thought of Thoreau's words, "If a man does not keep pace with his companions, perhaps it is because he hears a different drummer. Let him step to the music which he hears, however measured or far away." It was definitely a different vacation, but one I would repeat in a drum beat.

Grandma's Visit

The odds were in our favour. There were five of us. There was only one of her. My grandmother had agreed to manage the household while my parents went on a well-deserved vacation to Mexico.

Grandpa didn't join her in her volunteer mission. He'd probably heard the family stories.

On one occasion the mailman had carried home the twins while on his route. At their rolly polly age of three they were like two squirming, squealing piglets under each arm. His mail sack was around his neck and he was almost bent backwards with all the extra weight. James and Bruce had wandered off and he had managed to round them up to return them home. The rest of us hadn't noticed their absence.

I was too busy stepping in wet cement sidewalks that had just been paved by the City workers, sitting on fences that had just been painted, or plucking the tops off tulips from the neighbour's garden. Once my best friend, Terry, and I skipped off to the shopping mall which we knew in our five-year-old hearts that we shouldn't do, but the thought of Popsicles on an overheated summer day was stronger than our guilt. I was punished for that one. It was in the days of spankings. I did get to choose my torture. I opted for staying in my room all day. Terry got both the slap and the solitary confinement.

My older brother and sister did their share of upsetting the family circle of harmony by punishing each other. Robert locked Joan out one night. She came home from skating with no way of getting inside. She sat on the porch in below zero freezing weather waiting for my parents to return from their dinner out. My mom still chills up when she remembers the story.

Although Grandpa wasn't willing to submit himself to the unknown mischief we might get into, Grandma was a fearless lady. She had helped keep her home during the Depression by earning money babysitting.

She carried a frail frame. She tended to tame us with her tender touch. I, for one, expected little change in my life with her arrival.

There was a routine. She would need to follow it. While walking home with grandma returning from our walk to the grocery store, I asked the usual question.

"Can Terry stay for lunch?" I expected no resistance.

"No, dear, we have to get lunch for enough mouths. Terry can come another day."

"But mommy always lets him," I said.

"Well, mommy's not here."

This wasn't the way it was supposed to be. I decided I couldn't tolerate such ungrandmotherly behaviour. I ran off, hearing my grandma's voice disappear behind me.

"Kim, come back," she cried.

I had the advantage. I wasn't carrying bags full of groceries, like Joan and Rob or pushing a stroller, like grandma. I arrived home enough ahead of everyone that I was able to hide. I chose my brothers' closet behind all the clothes. I even put on my older brother's shoes so if anyone looked in they wouldn't see my sandals.

I could hear Terry's little voice talking to my grandmother.

"If anything happens to Kimmy, I don't know what I'll do. "

My twin brothers started giggling.

"It's not funny," said my grandmother.

"Do you think she could have fallen down a well? Terry asked.

"I think it's time you went home for your lunch. We'll let you know when we find her."

She opened the front door. Grandma recruited Rob and Joan to help. Rob took his bike to return to the store looking for me.

Grandma's voice had gone up an octave as she called my name. She and Joan looked under every bed, behind the couch and in the bathtub.

James and Bruce got up from playing with their toys on the floor. I don't recall if it was the tone of alarm coming from their throats or their investigative skills that found me, but I wasn't lost for long.

My grandma was not the kind of person to stay angry. Instead of scolding me, she hugged me.

"Please don't do that again," she said.

And I didn't. I decided that maybe it was more important to get to know her than include Terry at the lunch table. It's my only recollection of grandma looking after us.

Pampered in Madawaska

August 12, 2011

We are back at Madawaska this year. It's lovely to be loved and pampered the way we are when we are invited to Madawaska. There is something about these Madawaska adventures that always remind me of an Agatha Christie mystery. We are thrown together with new and interesting strangers in a log cabin palace, a wilderness experience with great white pines, canoes, kayaks, loons cooing in the distance and boating excursions. It is both relaxing and entertaining. This year the cast of characters have some from the past (Naomi, Marie and Murray) with new people Granger (Genny's uncle), Heinke (a broker from Germany who does a lot of work for monks), Melissa (a woman from Portugal who is friends with Genny), Jill (a long-time friend of Genny's), and last but not least there is Carmen and of course Peter and Camilla are the perfect hosts.

We had a moment of concern coming when our car broke down on the side of the highway. Fortunately, we were in front of a man's house where the owner knew all about cars. We were near Madoc. Instead of having to return to Brighton, he was able to take out his tool box and fix the car lickety-split. It turned out just to be a lose sparkplug. He would not even take a few dollars as a tip.

We made it to Bancroft in fairly good time and took the time to stop in Maynouth to buy some Canadian pottery – one of our guilty pleasures. On vacation we tend to forget about budgets. I guess in some ways we feel we are so blessed with this wonderful free vacation of being treated like royalty that we spend money as if we were rich.

The longest part of the trip seems to be the stretch from Maynouth to Barry's Bay. The second longest is the road to the log cabin resort from the Madawaska turn off. One has to get to Victoria Lake and then drive around the lake until one cames to the hill that winds down to the rushing water, a river spilling dramatically from the black depth of the lake.

Genny met us and we instantly felt right at home. Peter and Camilla came out next and encouraged us to make ourselves at home which we immediately did. We went for a swim and then sat around on the grand porch becoming reacquainted with everyone.

We had a lovely dinner of shepherd's pie, salad and brownies for dessert. Eating here is always like being at a five-star restaurant. We sat around the fireplace after dinner, just talking and laughing.

August 13, 2011

I gave Tai the wrong breakfast time and we showed up 20 minutes late. (Why didn't I check with someone!!!!?) Peter and Camilla were very forgiving.

My chat with Grainger reminded me of my wonderful grandfather. He regaled me with story after story. Camilla filled in some missing gaps and winked at his hyperbolic nature.

Mark, Peter's nephew, arrived with his daughter, Jane. He is the builder that we've met at various family events. There was the time we went to the Grafton Inn Christmas and the party at Peter's home at Christmas. I asked him how the project in Cobourg was going and discovered a business venture that went wrong. He joyfully said he recovered. I am such a nosey parker, I asked more questions than I should have so I let it go.

The weather was a little overcast so everyone went to their rooms with a good book to have a snooze. I worked on a Bible lesson plan for the next day and ended up sawing logs.

After my snooze I came out to the porch to enjoy tea time and chatted for a bit before going in to the dining room to enjoy a lovely roast beef dinner. It was the kind of beef that melted in your mouth. We all stayed around the dining room table telling stories and laughing until it was just the lantern light that lit our way to see the glorious stars sprackling in the heavens. I had a lovely chat with Peter about the Grafton Inn. We all turned in fairly early.

Sunday, August 14, 2011

We had a swim in the morning before our banana pancake breakfast. We went for a walk to the farm that isn't there anymore. The mosquitoes were fairly thick and hungry so we hurried back to a have a church service by the fire. I read a few passages from the Bible about God the creator and then a few passages from *Science and Health with Key to the Scriptures*. Genny shared some questions about eternal life and then we sang hymns for almost an hour.

We abundantly realize how fortunate we are to be here. Like the cousins who come once a year, we too, get to come for a visit. We have none of the organizing or even discussions about what needs to be done. We simply get to savour the gourmet meals and the warm chats with the other guests.

I write this while sitting on the front deck looking out to the expansive wilderness vista of trees that stretch into Algonquin Provincial Park with the small white cabin, way off across the bay, in the distance peeking out of the bushy green. The lake is quiet this morning, almost as still as glass. There is a mouse under the deck that is chomping on something so that now and again it sounds like he is trying to break out of prison.

Tai and I sat holding hands for a few minutes and then all of a sudden it was time for lunch, tacos galore. I worry about appearing too much of a piggy so I have to watch how much I eat.

How God blessed we are to have such wonderful friends and a wonderful view. Thank you Genny, Peter and Camilla. We love you.

The World of Apples and Apple Pie

With 7,500 varieties of apples in the world, which one did Eve give to Adam to eat? Or even more important, which one would she have found best to use to make an apple pie? And what is the secret to making a great apple pie?

There was no point in looking back into my own culinary experiences to come up with the answer. When it comes to cooking, I take after my aunts. Either I end up doing some fool thing like Aunt Helen who allowed her cake to drop off the windowsill where she put it to cool. (And that wasn't the worst part; she ran down three flights of stairs, picked it up, and still served it to her guests for supper.) Or else I cook like my Auntie Marg who was always looking for the easiest, rather than the most mouth-watering recipe for the family reunion. One year she brought raspberry Jello filled with canned tomatoes (I'm not making that up. And it tasted just the way it sounds).

No, for tough questions like those above it is best to ask the expert. And who knows more about making homemade apple pies than "Mom?" I asked her if I ever made apple pies with her when I was a child.

"Land sakes, no way," she said. "Making apple pie is a one-person job. You have to work quickly. Children play with pastry as if it was Play-doh. There is nothing that makes a pastry more difficult to work with than if it has been tossed around by hot little hands. It's time you could cook."

"Can I just follow the recipe on the Betty Crocker website?"

"Not if you want to make a really good pie. Betty Crocker doesn't tell you all her secrets or you could make pie as good as she. And then how would she become so famous? For example, on her website, she tells you to 'jump start your pie by using a Betty Crocker pasty mix.' Why, I never heard of such a fool thing, as making a pie with a pie crust mix. That's one step away from store-bought. When it comes to pie making, that's a might more than a 'jump-start.' That's starting the engine in third gear."

"Also Betty tells you to use 5 cups of peeled apples, but she leaves out the most important secret the kind of apple. Delicious apples don't break down well and they don't have as tart a flavour as the McIntosh. I have found that while the Empire (a McIntosh/Delicious hybrid) might be tastiest for eating raw, I use McIntosh for cooking apples sauces, crisps, pies and butter. Also don't store your apples on the sideboard. They might look lovely, but overripe apples give off ethylene gas causing other apples to ripen too quickly and spoil. (Use the overripe apples for your apple sauces.) Apples ripen 10 times faster at room temperature. So keep them in the fridge where, in perforated plastic bags, they can keep up to a month."

"Cold" is the key to good pies especially when it comes to the pie crust."

"Everything must be cold. Don't be trying to make a pie on a hot humid day. You'll be starting with everything working against you, if you do. Make sure all your ingredients are cold. Before you start, put everything in the fridge, even your rolling pin. Your Aunt Bet used to run her hands under cold water before she started." (I wasn't sure I wanted to trust an aunt, so I ignored that comment.)

"Because you're short like me, don't put the bowl on the counter for mixing because you are always reaching up over the bowl. Put the bowl in the kitchen sink so you are reaching down into the mixture, turning the bowl with your hand as you mix."

"Wouldn't it be easier to use your mix master to blend the pastry?" I asked.

"Give me strength. You really don't know anything about baking do you? That would make your pastry all flaky bits. Making pastry is like painting a watercolour. You have to work quickly, but gently. Remember the good MRS, Mix, Roll and Spread. Divide your pastry mixture in half so that while you're working with the bottom pastry, the top can be staying cool in the fridge. Place the bottom shell in the pie plate pushing gently so you don't create holes."

"I sprinkle a little bit of white sugar over the pastry bottom and when I've put all the apple slices in, I daub a ¼ cup of brown sugar and ¼ cup butter on top before putting on the pastry lid."

"No wonder your pie always tasted better than the neighbour's."

"One last final bit of advice. Be careful where you put your pie to cool."

"Not on a window sill?"

"No. One time when I had just finished getting you and your older brother and sister off to school, the twins played quietly on the kitchen floor while I made a pie for supper. I took a break in the living room to read the morning paper. The twins weren't old enough to talk yet but I could hear 'hau, hau,' sounds coming from behind the kitchen door. I leaped up from my chair, worried that I had left the oven on and they had opened the door. There was James standing on top of the baby table that he had pushed over beside the counter. His hands were covered in pie. He had shared his findings with his brother who was covered in clumps of pie. Bruce responded with 'hau, hau' each time he was pelted with more pie. So you do need to be careful there is no prey in the way of where your pie cools."

"Thanks, Mom. And do you know which apple Eve gave Adam?"

"It might not have been a apple. The Bible refers to it as the "fruit of the tree;" it never calls it an apple. It was probably some writer like John Milton with his Paradise Lost that referred to it as an apple. And I should also tell you that Betty Crocker is not a real person. She was a great marketing tool for a company who sells baking products.

Why is it that moms know everything?

Art Watershed

When fear started There has been concern that the arts could disappear from the school curriculum because it is too costly. Studies have proven that the arts are important to a student's education in teaching confidence, coordination, cooperation, culture and ... From the mouth of babes we discover what part the arts play in children's lives.

Talking to seven-year-old Patrick we find the essence of art in a child's life. "Having fun. I like to draw knights and Spiderman."

Marie, his 13 year-old-sister defines the arts. She divides the arts into two categories, the visual and performing arts. She provides her own dictionary definitions. Music: "It's kind of something magical that you can't see but you can hear. And it sounds beautiful most of the time." Dance: "A form of life. It's movement. It's so amazing what dancers can do." She compares a dance performance to a thunderstorm. Drama: "It's being someone who you aren't. For example, in the Roman time, I think, boys acted girls." Visual art: Drawing and painting "It could be displayed like a photograph but a lot more work goes into it, like it might take a long time to paint a picture but it doesn't take long to just click a camera. You can also paint things that you aren't able to see. For example, I might not be able to go to Japan to see cherry blossoms, but I can still paint them."

Sixteen-year-old, Joelle sees the arts as a way of learning about other cultures. As a dancer she has been impressed by the African tradition in the dances that she learns. "You read about plays about countries that."

Joelle, who used to be quite shy, has benefited by her dance performance. "Dance and drama are good because you get more confidence. You perform so much that you're not conscious that you're performing. That self-consciousness fades away."

"Art is a form of expression of their ideas and thoughts. It amazes me to see them play the piano." Bruce "Parents love to see their children perform."

"When we went to the Santa Claus parade. There was a phenomenal number of dance clubs. Every second float was a dance club. You know what the kids are doing here after school." Wendy

"It teaches you about individual expression. Some people are comedians and some people are Shakespearean actors. There is a plethora of expression and you don't have to be the same as someone else." 21 year old

Escape

"Please, you've got to tell me."

"I know you know where they've gone."

"You were the last person that saw them."

"And don't tell me you don't know. Your article in the newspaper told everyone how unhappy they were here at Lockwood Lodge. But how was I to know? Do you know how badly my parents communicated with me? No, you wouldn't because you never asked me. You just wrote your story from what they told you. Do you know how hard it was to find Lockwood Lodge? Do you know that I went with my father to every nursing home in this city? It wasn't easy. Do you realize that many of these places would have separated my father and mother not only separate rooms but they would have lived on separate floors. My mother needs some care. She can't get around on her own, and, unfortunately, my father can't face the fact that he isn't able to look after her by himself."

"How dare you say that? That I would be waiting until they're gone so I could have their money? Did they tell you that? Did they also tell you that they I'm paying for Lockwood Lodge because they can't afford it?"

"Look, I know you think I've stuck them in this home because I don't want to look after them. But the truth is I can't. My business demands that I travel a lot. I'm an only child. There is nothing else I could do."

"So don't tell me again that your journalism ethics won't allow you to tell me where they are. And I know you know. The photo that ran in the paper shows them walking out of Lockwood. If you didn't know where they were going then why didn't you run a picture of them sitting in the lobby where you interviewed them? No, they told you what they were doing and so you took that pathetic picture of them walking down the hall, probably out the door on this freezing cold November day. Did you also notice they only had their nighties on?"

"It infuriates me that you suggested I'd put them in a prison. If it's a prison I've put them in then you must realize they are like two budgies. If you let them out on their own in this world they won't survive a night. And that's why you have to tell me."

"So please, tell me where they are."

"On their way to Cuba? They don't even like the sun. Thank goodness, I still have time to get them at the airport before they go. You're a good writer, but make sure you get the facts next time."

Wedding Day

It were a stinking hot day, but Amy had wished for it to be sunny on her weddin' day and it sure enough was. There weren't a cloud in the sky. I think it were the hottest day of the year. I can member it 'cause I had to wear a suit an the tie around my neck felt like a noose ready to stop my breath at any moment. Don't know how fellas wear these things every day of their lives. Probably half the reason when you're a business boy that the homestead seems so comfy when you get yourself home. Ya get to free yourself. Ma keeps tellin' me I'm going to have to wear a suit all the time if I decide to go into business an' move to the big city. It's enough to keep a fella on the farm.

Amy had wakened early and was sittin' on the porch sewing some last minute girly thing a veil to wear on her head. Ma said she didn't think she'd slept a wink 'cause her bed didn't looked slept in. No wonder this was supposed to be the most special day of her life. I think Amy was a might nervous. The reason I knew this for a fact is that ma tried to take a picture of her in her weddin' dress when she had the veil all fixed and she was standin' out back in the garden beside the fish pond. I knew she must be quiverin' inside when she stumbled and went into the pond with her weddin' dress and all right up to her knees. Ma got so excited I thought she was going to stumble right over her and end up in there with her. But that was only the beginning of the things that could go wrong on this special day.

When Ma went inside with Amy and tried to grab the hair dryer from Cath. She almost had a fist fight. Ma kept yelling at Cath to give her the dryer and Amy just stood there frownin' as if it was her funeral, instead of her weddin' day. When Ma finally got the hair dryer she put it on full power against the dress and must have short-curcuited it on somethin' 'cause it plumb went totally dead. Then she got out the Hoover and tried blowin' warm air on it, but that only blew around a bunch of red fluff from the carpet so that it left little red specks over Amy's pretty white dress. I thought Mama was goin' to cry. Amy was kinda numb so we didn't see much emotion at all from 'er.

My sis, Cath, was bound and determined to find a new man at the weddin' so she was twirling and curling her 'air and putting so much make-up on that no one would recognize her. Probably a good thing. 'Cause those who had been victims in the past might go fer her all over gen, thinkin' she was a new girl in town. Or maybe she figured if her face was all dolled up, no one would notice the rest of 'er. Her red and white checked dress was enormous. She had taken it to the dry cleaners last week and the lady behind the counter apologized that they didn't dry clean tablecloths. Just as she said that she noticed the zipper in the dress and tried to excuse herself. But it was too late, Cath walked out of there fuming as if the lady had committed a terrific sin. I thought it was funny myself and made the mistake of snickering when Cath told about it at the dinner talk that night. Pa gave me the sternest look and I turned back to my neeps and tatties and said not another word.

Cath was Amy's whole weddin' party besides me of course who was the best man. I liked the "best" part most, even more then I liked bein' called a "man." Johnny used to call me "Squirt" when he was first courtin' Amy. But he'd grown to respect me, probably 'cause I know how late he'd bring Amy back home sometimes and I didn't squeal to ma an Pa none.

Johnny was a swell guy. His real name was Jacques 'cause he came from Quebec. But no one in these English parts ever call him that. He was a hard worker and we could all see that. He has a good job at the Abitibi mill in Iroquois falls foreman they called him, whatever that means.

I wasn't quite sure how all his kin folks were goin' to fit in at the weddin' because half of them only spoke French and most of us only spoke English. But as luck will have it, Amy had studied French for four years in University so was well prepared. 'Course she was goin' to be busy with a heap of other things so I'm not sure she would be able to do much translating.

I'd made sure I learned a few words in French, too nothin' bilangual, but I made sure I could say "bonjour" and "au revoir" and that's all I really felt I needed in the case as I met some sweet Quebecois girl. I remember my two buddies from school who went to Quebec for a summer vacation and when they came back from Trois Riviere I asked them what they'd learned. "Laitue" an' "poulet" they told me so I figured they must be two very important words. So you can imagine my disappointment when I found out that they meant lettuce and chicken. I wasn't sure how that helped you survive in a foreign land.

Johnny had planned most of the weddin' 'cause that's just he way he was. He knew what to do and Amy hadn't been to a lot of weddin's. She told him he could range everythin' and she would be there. That near sent Ma round the bend, but I think Amy was smart doin' that 'cause she knew that if she left things to Ma there might not be a weddin'. The only task Johnny gave her was to 'range for a fotographer. She done that. She asked her cousin Herbie to take all the pictures and though he said he'd do it, come the weddin' day he never showed up. We never did find out what happened to him. Cousin Clyde said he 'magined that Herbie had got a better offer some place else that was actually going to pay for his services.

So everythin' was now ready. Johnny was right calm for someone bout to commit himself for life. I hope I'm as cool on my weddin' day. He asked me where the flowers was for the church. That was Cath's task. Turned out she'd asked cousin Anthony to get the flowers. Anthony lived two hours from the farm so when he stopped at the side of the road to pick up a batch of wild flowers for the weddin' his car was already overheating with air conditioner and havin' it sit idle with his ma in it while the kids picked the flowers, caused it to overheat so bad that there was no way of cooling anyone when they realized they was going to miss the weddin' procession.

We waited as long as we could. Johnny looked so noble standing so straight, like one of my toy soldiers. I must admit he looked so nice and bronzed that I felt a slight enemic like a white perch. I guess working out in the wilds had given 'im a nice brown colouring.

Cath kept smiling sweetly to the minister, as someone had made the mistake of telling 'er that he was single. Truth was he been married for 20 years.

Finally the organ started playin' and everybody stood up. Amy came down the aisle so dignified that she could have been a princess. I was so proud of her. Pa looked a might nervous as she held on tight to his arm. And of course there was Little grams trailing behind them both. The minister had said anything could happen during the ceremony but the ushers were not to let anyone come down the center aisle after the bride. Wouldn't you know little grams must have been so low that the ushers missed her. She was bent over fixing Amy's train and I guess she didn't know quite where she was going. When she finally straighted up she was at the front of the church. She didn't know what to do. She sneaked a peak on the other side of Amy and the minister looked like he'd just seen a ghost. I know they talk about hail and brimstone sometimes and we almost had it right there and then. To me, I couldn't see what it mattered but I guess the minister was the finicky type that had just one rule and ya weren't supposed to break it. Uncle Eugene stepped out of the aisle and grabbed her and squished her in between him and Aunt Pat, while a soft snickering sound filled the church.

Yuletide Yarns and Department Store Blunders

We humans are such crazy creatures. Instead of being clever like bears and hibernating for the winter, we venture out into sub-zero temperatures to do our Christmas shopping. The downtown core of Toronto is almost always chockablock with people, but today—less than a few days before Christmas—it was as if the Blue Jays had won the World Series again. I put on extra padding not just to keep warm, but to protect myself from the shoving and bumping I most often experience in the subway.

It was like experiencing human bumper cars as you ran into people shopping along the aisles of toy town. It's not just physically exhausting; it's also mentally absorbing. It takes a lot of thought and memory to buy the right Christmas present. I had a slight advantage—I have a crystal-clear memory from my childhood to help me choose presents. I remember receiving a dress the colour of the underbelly of an old rusting car. It was adorned with the biggest, most grotesque white plastic elephant belt buckle—and wouldn't you know it, there was no way of detaching the belt from the dress. At that moment, I made a vow: I would always buy toys instead of clothes for children.

When buying gifts for grown-ups, I learned fairly early not to trust my grandmother Maben's advice. She told me that the best method of gift-giving was to buy a present I would like someone to give me. After the second Christmas of giving my father a Betty Crocker bake set, I was gently encouraged by my mother to rethink my strategy.

One year, my brother James and I were determined to complete our shopping in record time. We headed to Simpson's. Those were the good-old days when department stores were laid out in a grid format, so it was easy to find what you were looking for. Of course, the word we were looking for to aid us in our shopping spree was "SALE." I saw the word in large, bold letters off in the distance, dangling over a floppy bin of sweaters. It seemed to me the sweaters were a good buy—only $19.99. A sweater would be just the right gift for my dad. James and I proceeded to shuffle through the pile.

"Oh my gosh. Is this one ever ugly!" I mumbled, only slightly under my breath, as I remembered my elephant-belt-buckle dress.

Like the dress, the sweater was the colour of the underbelly of a car—but even worse, a car that had splashed through a mud puddle. I held it up at arm's length and waved it at my brother so he could get a good look.

"Have you ever seen such an ugly sweater, James? Who would ever buy such an ugly thing?"

As I turned to toss it back in the bin, a stranger was standing in front of me, holding a very attractive purple V-neck sweater that would be perfect for my father.

"Excuse me, miss—that's my sweater."

I quivered and glanced over at James for some assurance. I mouthed the words, "He didn't hear what I just said, did he?"

My brother hardly said a word. With a smirk, he nodded. "Yes."

With bashful eyes, I handed the man his sweater. I wasn't sure what the interplay was going to be. I expected him to scowl at me and stomp away, but instead, he must have felt some sympathy for my awkwardness. He gave me a big smile in exchange for his sweater. As he walked away, he said, "My daughter gave it to me last Christmas."

Tribute Writings
to Kim

Miguel Ángel Olivé Iglesias

Hail Kim

(in collaboration with Alina González & Jorge Pérez)
To Kim, with gratitude

Hail Kim, full of grace,
Tai is with you,
blessed you are among Canadian women
and blessed is the fruit
of your creative writing, poetry.

Holy Kim, mother-in-poetry,
help us writers
now and in the hour of
our publications.
Amen.

The Lady of the Winter Video-Words

Three or four poems by Kim Grove
were enough for me to feel serenity
from those idyllic-landscape kind of movies
she gently taps into computer video-words.

I am not acquainted with snow; winter is alien to me;
but the Lady of the winter video-words
features it for me. I sit and read (watch)
menagerie swaying with the gentle icicle breeze
or posing photographically vulnerable to Kim's sensitivity.

There are oozing shadows and damp fleeting noises
in the movies that she wondrously edits and reedits
so winter is no longer a stranger to my eyes.
Kim collects it in cozy glass igloos
tenderly allowing the sleet to shower them with tidbits of frost,
the winter video-words enriching my repertoire of experiences
and "winterness" inlaying itself somewhere into the surface
of my Cuban mostly-summer mosaic.

Tai and Kim

I am Tai's wingman and Kim's brand-new friend,
they have accepted me in their already
ample circle of trust and acquaintances
they have providentially touched with their
genuine laughter, forthright eyes
and feet-on-the-ground generosity.
Tai is a bulky Canadian, very impressive
despite the verdicts of a disappointed Gibara boy
("That's the Canadian who saved Jorge??!!").
He is talkative, friendly, open-hearted,
(he owes me a million dollars, says he
will pay me "tomorrow" trying hard to turn
the tables I won't budge). Tai displays a powerful
voice that he modulates at will at Jorge's home,
captivating us all with his stories and his love-packed
chatting that he accompanies with a zillion petabytes
of hugging and joking ("My Wingman, I'll punch
you in the vomer!") and laughter and good will.
Tai is "Tai-ed" to Kim, his love;
I dare say his alter ego. In them, harmonies
of liveliness and serenity are at home,
we all look up to them with pleasure
and benign envy, because we know
God smiled on them and blessed their union.
Kim is a gentle Canadian flower,
sweet, calm, knowledgeable.
She pays attention to your words with committed,
welcoming eyes that give you peace
and make you feel so comfortable.
Tai and Kim beautifully complement each other
complementing our lives by extension,
planting so much hope, certainty
and friendship as they fill those
spiritual voids (we sometimes collapse into)
by offering a helping hand, a revitalizing embrace,
and Tai's frangible promise to me
of a million-dollar recoup!

The Uninvited Season

[title taken from Richard—Tai—Grove]
(to Kim Grove, in memoriam)

Inevitable, grey, ominous,
a season sneaks in bringing
ice that intends to frost,
voids that pretend
to unfill the sweet memory
and the now wanting spaces.
The season of absence
that pierces the hearts
of many; the season of why's
echoing and consuming;
the season of crushing grief
for which no RSVPs would
have ever been sent, yet it came
anyway—uninvited.

John B. Lee

Every So Often

for Kimberley Elizabeth Grove

the day the news of your passing came
the orchid
you gave us
several years ago
bore seven blooms
every so often
it lost the light
and dropped its withered petals
to the pot
like the falling there
of beauty into darkness
we dutifully cared
for want of faith in future flowering
though it
thinned down to a single lonesome stem
green wired to the leaves
we pampered it with ice
set like vanishing jewels upon the earth
where the roots drank
meltwater slow
as with the expertise of forest spring
the winter went away
as sunlight sorrows into night
like frost releasing heat
and if the soul is real
within the soil
and the heart's a seed
for breaking open
into truths of life
then by these fragile
blossoms you're known
in fragrant moments of renown
and by eternal rhythms of ethereal Mays
we're proven ever-present in our absence
evermore ...

Patrick Connors

Tribute
for Kimberley Grove

On the winding path of this life, we sometimes
meet people who make it straighter
or at least easier to get through.

While the rest of us make endless plans
these are the ones who make things happen
and go as well as possible in an imperfect world.

We are gathered here today
to support our good friend Tai, as we
celebrate the life of Kim, his better half.

It is difficult to understand why
people who make the world better have
to leave, but I take solace in our community.

So, let's remember to appreciate each other,
and join in raising a glass, as we pay tribute
to all our dear ones who have passed.

Kate Marshall Flaherty

A Mouse's Prayer

O constant moon,
you illuminate my tracks,
almost imperceptible
atop this thin blanket
of ice-crusted snow.
May you hide my scribblings
and nibbles
in shadowy corners,
and reveal for my shiny eyes
pearls of hard corn, crumbs
and paper boxes of flakes
I can gnaw holiness into.
Send a beam slantwise
into the farm window,
drench the dresser drawer's raggy nest
of tattered flannel
where my babes lie opaque
in woolen scraps;
where my warm lima beans
nestle together dreaming
six-small-parts-into-one
big mouse dream
of nut butters
and flecks of sharp cheddar.
I will scurry my prayer
across the stone mantel
beneath the clock:
My blessings on all cracks
and cubbyholes,
my thanks for all things small

and with seeds,
my wish for protection
from owl eyes and traps,
and things with lids.
O moon, you see me
when others do not,
you know my brown fur's sheen,
and you reflect for me
my own great smallness
in your immensely
dark and speckled sky.

Triptych for One Loon

I.
Loon on lapping Georgian Bay,
past the salt docks and raked sand.
Suddenly there, the bird
has bobbed up further
from where it plunged further
than imagined breath could be held.
Alone under the mid-day moon.

II.
Loon stays under so long
you almost forget he descended at all.
You turn back to your book on the beach
and then, like nostalgia, he comes
far from where you expected
he could go.

III.
Loon tilts his straight beak
and tucks his webbed feet for take-of –
flaps rhythmic wings that slap
down and up loon and his wavy mirror-twin
leaving
a lean V trail.

You can lie down now

In the dusk, a mauve-ink sky
smears down
to dark ground, settles.
Light the twisted wick,
leave its wavering glow
to the evening breeze—
it will falter and flame its way to wax.
Melt your body down,
rest in this shrine of stillness—
night birds
looning into silence.
Smell the darkening lake pines.
As your body surrenders
to the earth
your cot becomes an altar.

Donna Wootton

Cuban Wall

Come to the wall and wait.
We walk, Kim and I and pass many walls.
A wall rising from a mottled sidewalk
A privacy wall
A red brick wall
A terra cotta wall
We marvel at the wall topped by dark lichen,
the wall invaded by flowering plants.
the wall protected by a round tower.
We find one painted green and
there we wait.
Beyond is the ocean crashing into the sea wall.
Unlike the busy streets with long lines of Cubans
waiting to buy whatever is delivered,
it's lonely here.
This is where we'll swim.

Jorge Alberto Pérez Hernández

Where Are You?

for Kimberley Grove

You are there
In the blue fields of spring,
Where today the green leaves shine,
Which are lost in lush beauty
Where fresh lily sprouts
And a yellow crown are born
Full of white laurels.
Where the clear moans are heard
Of the wind that comes from the clouds.
There in that new world even the broken branches
That live among the ancient trees
Are full of love, peace and eternal life.
There you can hear the trills of love
Constantly repeated by light-winged birds.
There you can see the charming figure
Of the angels passing,
Singing sweet, appealing songs
Of praise dedicated to your new life.

Emma Kate Oswald

A Recollection

There's the spider. In the corner. There!
It's large and long and lanky.
It scared me half to death last night,
Beneath my warm wool blanky.

Could you evict it from the house?
We're all not brave enough,
And Daddy's on the island now,
Watching Terns and stuff.

She casually approached the thing,
And taking up a broom,
She carefully removed it from
The corner of the room.

"There's no need to be scared," she said,
"Of this cute little guy,
I'm sure we're less afraid of him,
Than he of you or I."

And then without a second thought,
She picked the spider up,
Took it out on to the yard,
Then let it scurry off.

And now the memory comes to close,
And in my mind I see,
This legendary human friend,
Of spiders and of me.

Jennifer M. Arnold

The Gift

Her eternal kindness flows through my heart
and that of my children.
Softening our view of the world,
Reminding us of all that is good.
A simple gesture, door always open,
A spider gently re-placed.
An item lent before we anticipated the need,
A problem solved before we had time to ruminate.
Her heart always open.
Selfless love leaves a lasting mark...
I am forever grateful.
I am forever changed.

Lisa Makarchuk

On Kim's Legacy

Your time here
Is a people's construct
measured in hours,
days and years
igniting creativity
inspiring and uniting
with life forces
of evolutionary processes
leaving behind
in their configurations
a loving, spiritual legacy.

You thus continue
in our minds, in our hearts
to build on memories.

Ontario's Northern Woods

Autumn preens
With bursts of reds
And orange and golds;
Primping crimson sumaches
Exact attention
Leaves of maples and birches
Splash their colours
Daring winter's embrace
To cover all with ashen blanket
Enshrouding verdant firs.
Above it all a chattering world
Continues its oblivion
While underneath fluffed white
Earthy hibernation
Intertwines itself
With leaves re-sustaining
From whence they've come
To nurture new life
Surging into being
To sprout its blossoming sprays
Of springtime blooms.

Upon the Condition of Ageing

Presence slowly fades
Into invisibility
Relationship threads
Imperceptibly fray.
A twitch, a twinge, a wheeze
Insinuate into muscles
Reminders that the motor
Is running down.
Passions fade; interests disperse
Ideas scatter; conclusions blur
A mere blip in history's wheel
Relentlessly lumbering forward
Its gears grinding thru the ages
Sowing new ideas as grist
For new generations.
Our bodies mingle
With a welcoming earth
For eventual return
To stardust.
And that's all there is.

Deb Panko

A Walk with Kim

The email from Tai that didn't 'kick back'
told me Kim had taken her leave from this place
we call home. I hadn't seen either of them
for a number of years, but still the news was

unexpected, hard to believe … and then a day
later a lost memory, more a visit with Kim
bringing Cuba with her. She is carrying a box
of baked goods, leading our group through

the streets of Havana, the hot sun saying
"Clothes can feel uncomfortable here
especially if you're walking far" far enough
to be a challenge and I'm not sure my legs

can manage a long detour, but Kim is cheerful
and confident. The box of baked goods in her
pair of steady hands, not exactly a gift and
definitely not a burden, holds my attention.

Her determination to carry it along one single
purpose of many seems to be Kim's way
of saying in the simplest language that each
detail, coupled with intent, will make a difference

down the road. During our visit, I can see
Kim's face clearly. She's smiling and I recognize
the musical tone of her distinct voice holding us
in this ever-present moment, a corner turned

the long distance wide open space now
a shared destination without knowing quite
how to get there, then to hear Kim reassuringly
say "I'm pretty sure it's this way."

Donna Langevin

Dancing

Kim, today my Mexican daughter-in-law
is teaching me to salsa in my living room.
I think of you in Cuba, fifteen years ago.
Wild about salsa,
you practiced with a passion
hotter than Habanero Chilli
or Camarones a la Diabla.

Like me, you struggled with basic steps
   pausing on beats four and eight,
    swinging your hips
   as your feet shifted weight.
Later, learning combos and circular patterns,
you mastered multiple Spot Turns
and seven ways to hold hands.

I dance in memory of you, Kim.

I'm sipping a mojito in Santa Maria del Mar,
   lauding you in Latin dance shoes
with suede soles and flared heels,
    free spinning
in our damp, dimly lit
   Russian Resort "ballroom"
to a recording by La Cara Band.

Now, may you salsa with souls of legendary singers
  on an ephemeral stage
    where you'll circle the stars.

May you open your arms, inviting us
  to dance with you through the cosmos.

Katharine Beeman

Four Seasons for Kim

Fall
Kim is
in the yellow leaves
gently drifting

Winter
Kim is
atop the crusty snowbank
frosted by the blue glow of evening

Spring
in the tender bud of a winged maple
twirling from the tree
Kim is

Summer
in the turquoise tide wafting
water to beach to water off Guardalavaca
boisterously greeted by beachgoing Cubans
is Kim

Kim
simply
is.

Anthony Di Nardo

On the occasion of a tribute
held to the memory of Kim Grove

Someone stood and said sandpapered
To mean a voice he heard from another room
And I knew whose voice he meant
We were a thousand strong in a room this big
Here to think and talk about how we remembered Kim
Her life for us reduced to words
Our bold, unwavering view,
both hers and ours, of how words work
to conjure flesh and blood
Her words like morning and afternoon resting at the open mic
Beads and pebbles, fossils to her name
Breakers on a human coast
Kim, who lived in nature lived here for just this day
Kim, who picked an orchid bloom
And gave each of us a leaf that fell to scoop a breath of air
Kim, her life in words
And birds that pulled on threads
Birds, like Kim, among the boughs that held those threads
And gave a warp and weave to a life in words
An orchid bloom in a Cuban garden
An orchid in the biggest room on Earth
When I think of Kim
I forgive the world its sins
And hear a kindness coming from another room

Miriam Estrella Vera Delgado

Guardian Angels

When the Lord needs guardian angels,
he chooses among us the very best.
That's why sometimes we are shocked
by the news of the passing
of someone very special.
We can't accept this kind,
sweet, understanding,
intelligent, supportive,
loving creature has left us.
But we must understand
that if the Lord needs guardian angels
he must take the very best of us!

Richard M. Grove (Tai)

The Kimless Minutes

As long as I keep
my head buried
in my computer,
in my writing,
in my photography,
in doing dishes
I am fine.
It is in the lingering
leaden light of a dawn
that never
seems to arrive,
when I come up for air,
that the Kimless minutes
wash over me
like a damp fog
that I can't
see through
when I mourn
that I have lost my love
someone to do
everything and nothing with.

Earth Bound

It is a still grey day
at Scarborough Bluffs
watching the vultures glide.

I wish I could soar like a vulture
silently stand on the air and gaze
beyond the grey horizon
looking for you on my
effortless, timeless slide
on the breeze of infinity.

The Umbrella Went Up

I fell in love with Kim
under an umbrella.
Before the umbrella
we were affectionate.
Before the umbrella
we were starry-eyed.
Before the umbrella
time was wonderful
and then on that fateful day
it rained.
The umbrella went up,
her arm linked with mine,
we dodged a puddle in unison
and then time stood still
as we fell in love.

Essays about
Kim's Poetry

About Kim´s poem
"Beckoned Into Dark Depths"
by Richard M. Grove

I hope it is not too presumptuous of me to present this delightful poem by my darling wife. I am proud of her poetry in how it often resonated with key themes in Canadian poetry, particularly the intimate and reverent relationship with nature. As you will have noticed, Canadian poets often explore a sense of belonging and identity through landscapes, wilderness, and the seasons, drawing on the vast, sometimes isolating yet profoundly comforting connection to the natural world. Kim and I shared a home in Presqu'ile Provincial Park just south of Brighton, Ontario. We had the privilege of walking out our back door into an almost wilderness with the song of calm. This poem captures that essence by depicting a quiet, almost sacred journey into the forest at night, where we often walked into the dark depth of forest quietude.

The use of vivid imagery, like the "black jewel" and "white clover of morning," Kim creates a sensory immersion that highlights the calm and majesty of nature—a common trait in Canadian poetry. This poem captures an almost devotional tone with the restorative nature of the land, suggesting a harmony that reflects many Canadian poets' environmental mindfulness.

I had the privilege of living this contemplative tone with my darling wife, coupled with the rich sensory detail day after day, night after night in Presqu'ile for almost 25 of our 31 years together. Kim's delightful poem, fittingly captures a distinctly Canadian appreciation for the quiet power and solace found in the forests of Presqu'ile. It was my privilege to share this landscape with her. The landscape and I will miss here depth and beauty forever.

Beckoned Into Dark Depths

The black jewel of this night is
shattered by full moon.
Long crisp shadows
guide our searching
tentative,
well placed steps
into the dark depths
of forest cover.

Our silent breath sings
the blissful song of calm
back to the whispering mist
that beckons us into the
cloistered silence
of our forest home.

This is where our
weekend hearts lie
soon to welcome in
the white clover of morning.

Intimate Strangers: the poetry of Kimberley Grove
John B. Lee

The first time I met poet Kimberley Grove she confessed a difficulty. We were walking along the beach near Guardalavaca, Cuba. My wife and I had accompanied a group of Canadians on vacation in a resort near the city of Holguín. We were a privileged few having only recently joined the organization known as The Canada Cuba Literary Alliance. My wife Cathy was walking ahead with founding member, Kim's husband, president Richard (Tai) Grove. We were staying at a resort called Hotel Tropicoco, a slightly rundown residence for tourists who might not be upset by the green-water pool and the world-weary ambience of a ramshackle place built on the water by the Russians whose architectural design created the appearance of a ship run ashore stranded on the coast overlooking the blue-green aquamarine waters of the Caribbean coast. Our entourage included about ten fellow travelers, mostly poets and at-the-time strangers who would bond over literature and the common appreciation of the beauty of the island and the quality of her people.

Kim and I were lost in conversation. Under a sun-blue heaven, we walked and talked of serious things. The day moon sat in the sky like a sand dollar tossed in the air. Like me, Kim seemed to enjoy meaningful and serious discussion of things that matter most in the world. It became clear to me that we shared a profound commitment to the act of creation. For her part, she stated unashamedly, and without a hint of sanctimony, the importance to her of her faith in God. And in so saying, she acknowledged that she did not feel capable of writing poetry that truly honoured her faith in the divine.

Who but Kimberley Grove might feel comfortable sharing such an intimate vulnerability as she did on that day of our first acquaintance. She was unpacking her heart and I was deeply honoured by her confidence in me, that I might not only listen, but also hear, and that I might not only hear but be thought of as someone who might offer helpful advice.

Her husband Tai, who has become a close friend over the years since that day on the beach, offered a workshop he called "Intimate

Strangers." In doing so he invited participants to consider a photograph and to look closely and think deeply and linger long enough for the image to yield up its secrets so that the image might inspire the viewer to write. I mention this workshop because it seems to me that Kim, although a stranger to me then, was one of those people blessed by possessing what Margaret Avison calls "the optic heart". In her poem Avison opines "the optic heart must venture," thereby risking the perils of revealing itself, though it reap the harvest by not only being seen, but of a kind of deep seeing unavailable to the careful hearted.

What did I say to her that day? I don't know that it was truly helpful, but it was received with the generosity of a studied and serious attentiveness. I reminded her of Emily Dickenson's advice to poets, "tell it slant." If you want to write a poem in which you honour your faith, don't try so hard. Surrender your intention. Let down your guard. Give up on your earnest desire to be profound. Give in and divine inspiration may come to you when you least expect it.

After that conversation on the beach, I wrote the following poem in an effort to show her what I meant.

This is What I Know of God
for Kim Grove

I sat and watched
a sand crab
in my footprint
by the sea.

And as I watched
the sand crab
I saw him
watching me.

Over the thirty years since then, my respect for Kimberley Grove has grown. I've read her poetry, and in it found a sincerity of intention, a simplicity of voice, a respect for the silence between words, and most importantly an appreciation for the commitment to improving the world by being true to what is best in us all, and that is the quality of soul that shines up from the pages on which her poems appear. In her case and by her example, she puts words into action by living a life that was true to the wisdom manifest in the profound connection between aspiration in writing and reification in life. In time, I've laid claim to the privilege of having been her friend. I've published her poems in anthologies, read her poems in print, and I can tell you, dear reader, if you want to know Kimberley Grove, especially those who never had the privilege of being in her company, you can rest assured that in her, there is no disparity between her words as they appear on the page and the life that she has lived in the world.

Here is a poem by Kimberley Grove that I included in my anthology *The Beauty of Being Elsewhere* (Hidden Brook Press, 2021):

Cuba

Is it the beauty of the country?
The spider top palms
Exploding everywhere,
Nature's fireworks
Or the rugged faces
That melt into sweet smiles
Or maybe it's knowing the sun
Is still alive
No, it is the kindness of
the Cubans that calls me back

After that walk on the beach, Kim came to sit with me one day over a meal in the restaurant at the resort. She expressed her gratitude for our "getting to know you" conversation.

I think here of the apostle Paul's letter wherein he speaks of the humble and the meek. In thinking about that phrase, I've come to realize that humility doesn't involve the denial of the talents you are blessed with, but rather to be truly humble you must be grateful for the abilities you are gifted with. Not prideful, but grateful. And by meek, I suggest that he might have meant shy of ego. Not that you are incapable of being dangerous to those who would do harm in the world. As it is with Blake's poems "The Tyger," and "The Lamb," those complimentary poems which tell of the seemingly paradoxical content manifest in the nature and character of Christ. To be fierce, and also to be meek in one incarnation. As it says in the Beatitudes, "Blessed are the meek." Blessed are those who are dangerous enough to be kind, when kindness calls you back to a land like Cuba, as seen through the eyes of the poet Kimberley Grove, where kindness is prized as a great virtue. The kind of kindness that shines forth in the closing words of Kimberley Grove's poem, "Cuba." It lives on in the pages of her work. It thrives as a beacon of the soul within and the spirit throughout. It is the dangerous kindness of fire in the light of her lines, the fire that lights the way, that keeps a comfort burning, and which like Blake's poems "The Tyger," and "The Lamb" answers the question: "Did he who made the lamb make thee?"

In Kimberley Grove's poems, even those with a less than obvious objective, like Blake she answers, "yes," and then again "yes." It is her faith in kindness, even in the dangerous kindness of fire.

A Review of Kimberley Sherman Grove's Poetics

Miguel Ángel Olivé Iglesias

One read of Kimberley Sherman Grove's poetry was all it took to captivate me and stir clear-cut images in my mind. I instantly called her "The Lady of the Video-words."

Talking to her was also an experience to cherish. The woman and the poet are one. She has an aura of sweetness and calmness that envelops you. I said: "Kim is a gentle Canadian flower, sweet, calm, knowledgeable. She pays attention to your words with committed, welcoming eyes that give you peace and make you feel so comfortable."

She lives with her husband, Richard Marvin Grove (Tai) on the shore of Lake Ontario in Presqu'ile Provincial Park, where they run a bed and breakfast for artists, writers and birders. The park is a great influence on her perception of the Canadian landscape. She walks out her back door into her poetry. I was lucky to read a collection of her poems, The Poetry of Kim Grove, compiled for the Canada Cuba Literary Alliance Cultural Festival in Santiago de Cuba in January-February 2010.

What I perceived was poetry as an extension of Kim's sensitive heart. She chooses her words carefully and holds them as a painter does with a brush: images spark out of it, flooding the reader's eyes. She is in love with nature, a theme deeply rooted in Canadian writers, but there is also the human presence as a beholder, or as a component of the picture.

When you read Kim's poetry you can feel a serene pat on your shoulder that registers in your brain thanks to what she offers: snowflakes of silence and quiet or white-vapor scurry-offs, or muffled hoof and paw sounds. We watch idyllic landscape movies she gives birth to and gently taps into computer video-words.

In "Nature's Needlepoint" she plays with images and sounds: "As the rumbling thunder like distant fireworks." Further below, Kim goes beyond by activating all senses: "Bright yellow daffodils worship the sun, while lilacs perfume the air. Roses, lilies and tulips sew more colour into the fabric." Spring is personified, in an intimate harmony of poet and nature: "She adds the hundreds of leaves that will crumple underfoot like worn paper bags. She applies some final touches, blowing away unnecessary edges or redoing ugly patches."

Nature is the protagonist. We also see the perfectionist in Kim Grove, the dreamer who can gild the view to ultimate exquisiteness. "Like worn paper bags" is a simile the poet handles so the reader, a stranger maybe, understands the natural wonders using a more "social" acoustic explanation, that of paper bags. Yet, Kim is not a stranger to her scenes; she is the messenger, the bridge that brings together nature and society. The tools are in her hands: she applies dabs across the canvas laid out before her: light slaps, gentle taps, fluorescent strokes that unfold the landscape for us, mesmerized "viewers."

In "White Menagerie," the poet takes pictures or videos the scenes: menagerie swaying with the gentle icicle breeze or posing photographically vulnerable to the poet's sensitiveness and sharp eye.

There are oozing shadows and damp fleeting noises in the movies that she wondrously edits and reedits so winter is no longer unknown to one's eyes. Kim has collected it in cozy glass igloos tenderly allowing the sleet to shower them with tidbits of frost that the reader feels. She marvels at the place she describes, and we marvel at the way she introduces her "explorer." She reaches up to kiss the man amidst a glorious setting, again the simile to fuse nature and society, "Creaking like Styrofoam under our feet," this time accompanied by onomatopoeia, "creaking."

"His Creativity" opens and closes with excellent lines. It is the apparently simple description of an intimate moment. It speaks between the lines of a gentle, sentient, valuing heart. "His creativity was in a fragile moment" is a euphemism that reveals the poet's state of mind.

The intricate, sometimes infinite paths of love are explored in "Falling in Love." The poet knows she will "slip off this thing" that is the red balloon of love, and complains she "should have got off a long time ago." But there she is, clinging to hope, to the experience, even in the dark notion that it all might take her to "have to live on a far off planet alone."

She is willing to take the risk anyway, so it seems.

Questions pop up: How and why did she get on the balloon in the first place? Isn't falling in love a human thing we must never give up, must strive for as many times as is necessary, and are entitled to?

In "Snow" the writer refocuses on one of her favorite motifs, nature. The poem stands on a simile: "like huge eiderdown pillows." I had already mentioned that Kim is able to translate into images what winter is. This poem continues the "didactic" endeavor of the poet, successfully. The "illusion of sugar covering the earth" reinforces my assumption of the sweetness in the poet´s heart and her penmanship to find the right words for the best of comparisons.

"The Challenge" is the endless battle of the mind and the physical part, the race against oneself, the test of natural instinct versus human psyche. Among the resources the poet wisely exploits are the expressive means of the language, turned into powerful stylistic devices: understatement ("a small thumbnail of a toad") repetition ("I´d" and "Of how…") skillfully handled to poke the readers´ capacity for patience, placing them in the poet's situation.

The poet defends the tranquility of the scene, the patience of the animal, as opposed to the "rush of the city," her own impatience, and leaves it to us readers to estimate how long she could really stand the test and check how many would turn and walk away.

One of the traits of Canadian literature is the observation of nature as a divine force that comes to us in splendid manners. Kim catches these manners and gives us a handful of images in motion.

Kimberley Grove sings to her Canada, that white Canada she sees from her cottage with an artist's eye. It is an array of images neatly, slowly, gently sketched; superb choice of words, divine success. The Lady of the Video-words has left us a gallery of images as impressive as the wondrous Canadian landscape they represent.

A Sliver of Divinity. A Review of Some of Kimberley Grove's Poems in The Divinity of Blue

Miguel Ángel Olivé Iglesias

In 2020 I published my first review book *In a Fragile Moment* (Hidden Brook Press). More than thirty poets and prose writers honoured it with their work. One of them was Kimberley Grove. About her, back then, I said, *"One reading of Kim's poetry was all it took to captivate me…"* Four years later I come back to her poetry, this time selecting poems from the Hidden Brook Press book *The Divinity of Blue*. The book, and its title (from one of Richard Grove's poems), is *"… is an homage to all of the beauty that we find in Cuba including its people…"* as Grove himself said in his introductory words. Many Canadian and Cuban writers joined in the celebration of a Canada Cuba Literary Alliance visit that turned into an excellent excuse to compile poetry written while being in Cuba.

Kimberley Grove sticks to the line of homage by filling her section with eight mostly Cuba-related, witty, funny, pensive and retrospective pieces, which will please the readers' expectations. Short and long poems adhere to the concept of enjoyment above all, of narrating and sharing with the readers the poet's experiences. The aim of *The Divinity of Blue* was to word the poets' myriad feelings and inspirations during their sojourn, mostly in Gibara, a coastal town north of Holguín City.

The poet's first proposal is "For my Husband." Precise, humorous and compact (two lines), the poem's fruitful impact is based on the *play on words* (I will explain this below),

> *Most men sleep with women*
> *My husband sleeps with earplugs*

Sleep with is a phrase with two meanings, at least in this poem: in line one, the presence of the prepositional phrase *"with women"* tells us the figurative sense of the sentence; while in line two there is a sudden deviation from the initial meaning. By adding a different prepositional phrase, *"with earplugs,"* which is more literal or direct. This handling of the language is achieved by a stylistic device I just mentioned above, play on words (also known as pun or double entendre). It works with the *"interaction of two well-known meanings of a word or phrase... Like any other stylistic device, it must depend on a context... Puns are often used in... jokes..."* (*taken from I. R. Galperin. Stylistics. Moscow Vyssaja Skola. 1981*). "For my Husband" is a good example of a pun put to jocose use.

"Cuba" is the poet's second proposal. It follows exactly Richard Grove's heartfelt statement about why they love Cuba and why the book came to life: Cuba's beauties and its people:

> *Is it the beauty of the countryside?*
> *The spider-top palms, nature's fireworks*
> *exploding everywhere in the landscape?*
> *Or the rugged faces turning to sweet smiles?*
> *Or maybe it is knowing that the sun is still alive?*
> *No, it is the kindness of the Cubans*
> *that calls me to return.*

In this case, Kimberley Grove uses a technique that will aid her in getting to the end answer. By asking a series of questions, she intrigues the readers and leads them down the poem, until in line six she opens her heart and provides *the* answer. Many tourists from abroad have fallen in love with our natural charms but also with the Cuban soul, where they find collective and individual virtues hard to come by anywhere else.

Overwhelmed by an unavoidable sentiment inherent in all humans, love, the poet presents "First Love." Kimberley tells us her own story, her seven-year-old experience, with skill and exactness. Underneath the lines, we pick hesitation, desperation, preparation, anticipation, anxiety, all of which hinge upon a little girl's innocent identification with what love should be like:

> *I saw it in the movies,*
> *so it must be true -*
> *a recipe for romance.*
> *I stood ever so silent*

> *in my backyard*
> *waiting....*
> *Short tiny breaths,*
> *knees like rubber bands ready to snap*
> *as I tiptoed on my seven-year-old toes*
> *to look through the crack...*

Excited by the moment, she describes a scene that is funny, throwing in movie terms as well:

> *I saw him approaching,*
> *a boy with sandbox blonde hair*
> *strolled along the path beside the road...*

> *Lights, camera, action.*
> *I ran to my father's rock garden*
> *sauntered among the*
> *daffodils, petunias, and tulips*
> *ablaze with colour.*
> *I conjured up my music teacher's voice.*
> *Echoing her vibrato, I sang*
> *a love song I had invented...*

Ah, that first-love instant, that flurry of emotions and confusions, was toned down in the end to:

> *I ran to see his reaction, but all I saw*
> *was the back of him, kicking a lone stone*
> *he had found underfoot.*
> *I stared until he was a speck in a cloud of dust.*

With the last line we realize that the girl had the patience to see her "love" walk away. He became a speck, so it took her time to say good-bye to him. That was the end of her love story.

Kimberley Grove is able to handle humour on various levels. "Our Cemetery" is actually hilarious. We are not aware of that until we reach the end line. Rather formal and familiar at the beginning, they are about to have a picnic,

The lion stood stone-faced
guarding the ancient mausoleum.
I was the height of my grandfather's knees.
He lifted me to pet the time-worn head of the beast
while my grandmother spread the patchwork quilt
on the velvety, freshly-mowed green grass...
...I eyed the plumb, moist chicken
that she uncovered from the picnic basket...

the poem turns very funny when we read about the mix-up. We cannot control our hilarity at the grandparents' utter confusion,

A small black jeep stopped beside us.
A stone-faced man yelled, "You can't eat here."
That day I learned that it wasn't our park.

It is only at the last line that we understand the situation. Kimberley continues to employ efficient techniques to keep the readers busy, interested and amused.

I immediately sensed a spirituality underlying our next poem. With that sensation, I also felt an aura of Eastern influence in the piece. I have not been able to find the haiku Kimberley's "The Wall" made me recall, but it presented a similar idea, that of a man whose house burns to the ground. Armed with his Asian wisdom and attitude before life, he comments that it is a good thing because now he can see the stars.

In my opinion, Kimberley suggests an analogous setting:

The yellow azaleas slip over the wall.
Purple moss drips over the edge.
Red bricks piled high, with
missing mortar coming loose.
How long have the bricks
withstood the aggression?
Is it time for the wall to crumble,
for the world to see the garden, the beauty
that is there and has always been?

A wall that must have had a role in the past is now hindering a better, higher sight. Kimberley activates anticipatory mechanisms in the readers by resorting to the "pre-view" wonders of the concealed spot she will introduce later, *"yellow azaleas."* She also enhances her poem with an expressive means in the language, rhetorical question (*"A statement expressed in the form of an interrogative sentence that requires no answer." taken from Villar et al. Exercises in Stylistics, Editorial Pueblo y Educación, 1984*). Rhetorical questions help *"… convey a stronger a stronger shade of emotive meaning."* (*taken from I. R. Galperin. Stylistics. Moscow Vyssaja Skola. 1981*).

While these questions are meant to have no answer, we are wisely informed by the poet—namely in the second question—what those wonders are. Within the structure of the question, Kimberley effectively manages to offer a peek (an answer) at the mystery entailed in the garden beyond the wall. It is an extraordinary poem.

I am closing my review with a poem about a distant location. Let's bear in mind that the poet is writing in Cuba, but her thoughts still travel to other realities she knows. "Mist" is somber, wistful, awesome and beautiful in its limning the vista she holds dear in her mind:

> *The mist hovers over the lake*
> *Weighing heavier with its thickness*
> *Leaving behind an offering,*
> *A comforting quilt of smoke*
> *Over past agonies, past wounds, past scars,*
> *Seeping into the harsh lines*
> *Scraping out the*
> *Cruel childhood memories,*
> *Left in rocks at*
> *The altar of Lake Memphremagog.*

The mist becomes an almost living entity with healing powers that leaves *"behind and offering, a comforting quilt of smoke…"* The poet is aware that *"past agonies, past wounds, past scars…"* must be left behind in the *"The altar of Lake Memphremagog"* and in the recesses of the brain.

This is the Kimberley Grove we read in *The Divinity of Blue*, a Hidden Brook Press publication in 2020. Her eight poems speak of her emotions, her experiences, her position in life and about life. A woman of modesty and tenderness, she reveals herself as a fine poet ready to see around her, capture the essences and pour them onto blank pages waiting for her. My quotation at the beginning of the review resonates loud and clear now that I have finished: *"One reading of Kim's poetry was all it took to captivate me..."* She has offered her fascinating sliver of divinity.

Afterword

Prof. Olivé, editor of *The Uninvited Season*, asked me to write a few words to close this fine book. I did not have the opportunity to meet Kimberley Grove; I had just heard about her through Prof. Olivé and her husband Tai. However, reading the book I have come to an understanding of who she was and how family, friends and acquaintances were touched by her marvelous presence.

Therefore, it is an honor to be the one to write these closing words and become a part of the many who, pained in the irreparable loss yet moved by Kimberley´s virtues and influence, offered their tribute to her.

Everyone called her Kim. May I say then that Kim is the light surrounding us today. She is now, as poet Miriam Estrella Vera Delgado says on page 103, so emotionally, a *guardian angel*. Thanks to Kim, Prof. Olivé tells us in his poem on page 83, I can "… *feel serenity*…" because that is Kim's warmth and peace caressing our minds.

I did meet Richard Grove (Tai), Kim´s husband, a few months ago in Havana. Tai and Kim visited Cuba together almost thirty times. During Tai's Havana visit I was witness to his unending admiration and profound love for her. We sat for hours and Tai would not stop telling me stories of their being together and of her being so wonderful and sweet. That is when I knew she loved Cuba very much, especially Havana. Kim participated in meetings in Havana for bi-cultural readings at the UNEAC Literary Garden and Havana University. For all that heard her, her readings were well received and respected. She also read at the International Book Fair in Havana. Kim was always a welcome presence in

Havana, particularly at Havana University. Both Kim and Tai went to Ciego de Ávila University as well to teach creative writing. Professors and students beloved her. Her joyful attendance, no matter where she was, adds to my appreciation as a Professor for having been invited to write this Afterword. I thank Miguel for inviting me and Tai for sharing so many emotional and heartwarming experiences of their life together.

In this way *The Uninvited Season* is an *invited season* of homage to a great woman whom I did not meet, but has turned out to be a gratifying memory, the writers in the book have helped me hold her in my heart.

Let me borrow Prof. Olivé´s customary ending words to his essays and reviews: *Thank you*, Kim, for who you were—and who you will always be for those who love you.

Full Professor Guillermo Ronda Velázquez. PhD
University of Havana, Cuba

Kimberley Elizabeth (Sherman) Grove

With the passing of Canadian writer, **Kimberley Elizabeth Grove**, we stand to honour her life and achievements. The list of family and friends that will miss her is far too long to list here. Suffice it to say that she was a beloved wife, sister, aunt, grandmother and friend to so many.

Though family was always a priority, Kim was not afraid to leave home for short periods to explore the world and other cultures. One of her first adventures was jumping on a train with a friend to cross Canada for a summer job at the Banff School of Fine Arts between high school and University. Taking a third university year abroad from her studies at U. of T. meant hopping on a Russian ship from New York to Southampton England to spend a year at St. Andrews University in Scotland. Later she took a year to teach English to Spanish students in Barcelona. She lived in Boston and Chicago working at the Christian Science Monitor and later at an architecture firm. All of these world adventures were followed by travelling with her husband Richard (Tai) to Germany, England, France, New Zealand, China, USA and Cuba (*Cuba over 25 times.*) over their 31 years of marriage.

She always made long lasting new friendships from around the world but always came home to spend time with family and friends in between these adventures. She was a true friend to all who had the privilege of knowing her whether briefly or over decades.

Kim loved nature, and in many ways, it inspired her writing. For almost ten years she and her husband owned two cabins in the middle of twenty-six acres of forest north of Barrie, Ontario. They sold that land and their Toronto condo and bought a house in Presqu'ile Provincial Park, where they lived for over twenty years. Surrounded by lake, forest, and wildlife, they ran a B&B. Kim, being such a generous and caring host quickly earned a "Best Host" designation from Airbnb.

Some might not know that Kim was a published author with a well-rounded writing career. She had a passion for writing from an early age, once stating, "I've been writing since the first time I picked up a pencil." Her enchantment with Cuba was deeply connected to her love of poetry, as she and her husband visited the island almost thirty times. Kim's work was published in *The Globe and Mail*, *The Christian Science Monitor*, *The Toronto Star*, as well as various smaller newspapers. She also worked as a reporter for the Community Press and *The Shield*, and was a regular contributor to *Watershed Magazine* and *Devour: Art & Lit Canada*.

Her latest book entitled, *Stories Inked*, was a commissioned manuscript for ORT Toronto. She was editor for the Canada Cuba Literary Alliance member anthology, *Sí Cuba* and was the substantive editor for a number of memoirs for individual authors including: *The Joy of Music*, and *Brothers Don't Fight*.

Her stories and poems have been published in numerous international anthologies, including, *Hola Cuba*, *A Time of Trial*, and *Grandmother, Mother and Me*.

Kim was the workshop leader for the Canadian Poetry Association, poetry and micro prose workshop and book publishing project entitled,

The Road Between The Years. She was also the editor, teacher, coordinator for the Brighton, Ontario library children's writing initiative entitled "The Family Flight".

Kim has been interviewed on radio and has written and performed eight radio commercials for the Grafton Village Inn.

She taught writing at Loyalist College, the Trenton Air Force Base, the Colborne Community Care Centre and Ciego de Avila University in Cuba. Her teaching came from a love of reading what others have to share. She was also included in many anthologies published by Hidden Brook Press and SandCrab Books.

Aside from Kim's memorable writing career it is equally important to mention that she was an active member of her church, First Church of Christ, Scientist, Toronto. Over her many decades of commitment she generously served on many committees including, the Distribution Committee, the Lecture Committee, the Benevolence Committee, the Usher Committee and at the church Reading Room. She served as the Church Manager for 13 years and also served on the Board of Directors. She was elected as First Reader for a three year term. Her long commitment to church was evident when she was appointed to be the Ontario Manager of the "Committee on Publication" reporting to the Mother Church in Boston.

"We were all deeply saddened to hear of Kim's passing. In thinking about her time with us, we are so grateful for all she did for this church—for her loyal membership, her inspiring testimonies, her faithful service in so many capacities—and, more than anything else, for her warm smile and uncountable acts of kindness."

May these heartfelt words pay homage to a generous, patient, smiling, beloved woman who lit up everyone's life with her presence.

Editor
Prof. Miguel Ángel Olivé Iglesias. MSc

About the Editor
Miguel Ángel Olivé Iglesias

Miguel Ángel Olivé Iglesias, MSc, born in 1965 in Bayamo, Cuba, graduated from the former Teacher Training College of Holguín. Associate Professor of Holguín University. He has a Master´s degree in Pedagogical Sciences.

He is the Cuban VP of the CCLA – Canada Caribbean Literary Alliance. He is a member of the Mexican Association of Language and Literature Professors, VP of the William Shakespeare Studies Center and member of the Canadian Studies Department of the Holguín University in Cuba.

He is a poet, writer, essayist, editor, translator and proofreader. He has published more than a dozen books including poetry and essays on CanLit. He publishes both academic and literary criticism papers and books, focused on the teaching of English as a foreign language and the analysis of Canadian literature, especially poetry.

He works in the Teacher Education English Department as a professor of English, English Stylistics and grad courses. He is also Head of the English Language Discipline. He uses his academic papers, essays, stories and poems in class for reading, debating and practicing the language, adding a didactic and formative element to his scientific and literary production. He also does poetry reading in co-curricular on-campus and community activities.

www.ingramcontent.com/pod-product-compliance
Lightning Source LLC
Chambersburg PA
CBHW051316120626
46547CB00015B/2268